Tillie Pierce

TEEN EYEWITNESS TO THE BATTLE OF GETTYSBURG

TANYA ANDERSON

Twenty-First Century Books • Minneapolis

To Eric Anderson, Dave Anderson, Dale Anderson, and
Dave Speas—the pillars and patriots of my life
                                                    —TA

Acknowledgments: With thanks to the Gettysburg Military Park/National Park Service, the Adams County (Pennsylvania) Historical Society, and the history-loving people of Gettysburg, especially Nancie Gudmestad (owner of the Shriver House Museum) and Gerry and Beth Hoffman (owners of the Jacob Weikert farm) for their help in making Tillie's story real to me.

Title page image: Wounded soldiers and medical staff pose for a photo at a field hospital in Gettysburg after the battle in July 1863.

Twenty-First Century Books
A division of Lerner Publishing Group, Inc.
241 First Avenue North
Minneapolis, MN 55401 U.S.A.

Website address: www.lernerbooks.com

Library of Congress Cataloging-in-Publication Data

Anderson, Tanya.
    Tillie Pierce: teen eyewitness to the battle of Gettysburg / by Tanya Anderson.
        p.   cm.
    Includes bibliographical references and index.
    ISBN 978–1–4677–0692–6 (lib. bdg. : alk. paper)
    1. Gettysburg, Battle of, Gettysburg, Pa., 1863—Juvenile literature. 2. Alleman,
Tillie Pierce—Juvenile literature. I. Title.
E475.53.A55 2013
973.7'349—dc23   2012018072

Manufactured in the United States of America
1 – DP – 12/31/12

Contents

Author's Note

WAR AFFECTS EVERYONE—YOUNG AND OLD, RICH AND POOR, WARRIOR AND PACIFIST AND, IN THE CASE OF THE CIVIL WAR (1861–1865), SLAVE AND FREE. Children and teens also carry the burdens of war, some as victims, some as child soldiers, some as gentle healers in their own communities.

In writing this book, I wanted to give a real voice—a teenage voice—to one of the most written-about wars in history. Matilda (Tillie) Pierce lived through the bloodiest Civil War battle. It took place in July 1863 around her hometown of Gettysburg, Pennsylvania. Tillie was fifteen years old at the time. She later wrote about her experiences in the 1889 book *At Gettysburg: Or, What a Girl Saw and Heard of the Battle, A True Narrative*. She is not the only eyewitness who wrote about the battle, but her story is one of the most compelling. I want people Tillie's age to learn about her and about the event that stayed with her the rest of her life.

This is not a book about the military details of the Battle of Gettysburg. Plenty of other books describe the battle's strategies and its leaders, the

Tillie
Pierce

winners and the losers. This book is about Tillie—before, during, and after the three days of battle in July 1863. I have included geographic, cultural, and historical information to help readers understand her place and time.

Few students have ever heard of Tillie Pierce. She was an ordinary teenager of her day who endured extraordinary difficulties. I want to share her story, using her actual words, so young people today can relate to one of the most important events in U.S. history. I want readers to see Tillie's courage, stamina, and compassion, so they can search for and discover the same qualities within themselves.

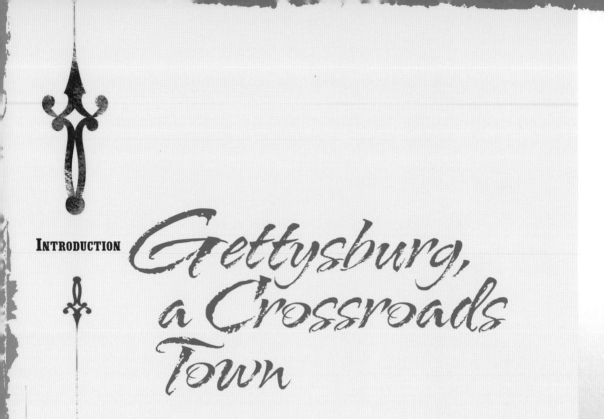

Gettysburg, a Crossroads Town

LONG BEFORE WHITE SETTLERS MOVED INTO SOUTHERN PENNSYLVANIA, NATIVE AMERICANS HAD WORN AN EAST-WEST TRAIL THERE. The path later turned into a well-traveled dirt road when French and English trappers ventured into the wildlife-rich Allegheny Mountains. Over time, another road developed. This one ran north and south, connecting Shippensburg (Pennsylvania) and Baltimore (Maryland). The place where these two roads crossed would one day be called Gettysburg.

In the 1730s and the 1740s, settlers who wanted nothing of city life in Philadelphia, Pennsylvania, and other large towns moved to York County in south-central Pennsylvania. They were hardworking, independent families who managed to turn the rock-filled, rolling hills into working farms. One of those areas was known as the Marsh Creek settlement.

Samuel Gettys, an immigrant from northern Ireland, was a settler there. He bought 381 acres (154 hectares) of the Marsh Creek settlement as a farmstead around 1740. In 1761 he built the Gettys Inn and Tavern near the crossroads of the town's two main roads. Gettys knew that weary travelers would be glad to pay for a place to sleep, eat, and drink. During the Revolutionary War (1775–1783), American troops found refreshment and rest at his inn.

In 1783 Samuel's son James bought 116 acres (47 hectares) from his father. James laid out a town on that parcel and named it Gettystown in honor of his father. He established a central square, known as the Diamond. Several streets splayed out from the Diamond like the spokes of a wheel. He divided the area along these streets into 120 individual lots. The streets were named to show where people were traveling to or from: Baltimore Street, York Pike, Harrisburg Road, Chambersburg Pike, Taneytown Road, and Hagerstown Road. People passed through Gettystown on their way to bigger and more exciting cities.

In 1800 the town's name was changed to Gettysburg, and it became the county seat. In a few years, two colleges were established northwest of town. Lutheran

James Gettys founded Gettystown in the 1780s. In 1800 the town's name was changed to Gettysburg.

This 1863 photo shows Gettysburg from Seminary Ridge.

Gettysburg was known for making carriages, including Conestoga wagons (below).

Theological Seminary opened in 1826, and Pennsylvania (now Gettysburg) College followed in 1832.

One of the main businesses in Gettysburg was carriage making. The area was well known for its fine horse-drawn carriages. It supplied a growing nation with all kinds of vehicles, including Conestoga wagons (also known as prairie schooners). Related businesses such as tanneries, ironworks, and blacksmith shops sprang up.

Outside the busy little town, farmers grew corn, wheat, rye, and hay. During the summer and fall, the bounty from apple and peach orchards kept families busy making apple butter and peach preserves. Some men ran still houses that produced gin, rye whiskey, and apple brandy.

TILLIE'S HOMETOWN

TILLIE PIERCE WAS BORN IN GETTYSBURG IN 1848. In her book, *At Gettysburg: Or, What a Girl Saw and Heard of the Battle, A True Narrative,* she describes Gettysburg as it was before the war:

> Prior to the battle it was comparatively unknown to the outside world, save to those interested in the Lutheran Theological Seminary here located. From year to year it pursued the even and quiet tenor [feel] of an inland town, with nothing

to vary the monotony but the annual exercises of the above-mentioned institutions. On these occasions the influx of strangers, for the short period of commencement week, did add some stir and life to the place, but only to have it settle into more irksome quietude [dull living] after the visitors and their dear boys had left.

At the time of Tillie's birth, Gettysburg was a farm-based community of about twenty-four hundred people. Its residents slogged through muddy streets and fields in the spring. Many had picnics and picked berries in the humid summer. In the fall, they harvested and preserved crops. During cold, snowy winters, they held one another close under handmade quilts and stoked fireplaces to stay warm. Tillie described some of these activities too:

> Often do I think of the lovely groves on and around Culp's Hill; of the mighty [boulders] which there abound, upon which we often spread the picnic feast; of the now famous Spangler's Spring, where we drank the cooling draught [drink] on those peaceful summer days. . . . What pleasant times were ours as we went berrying along the quiet, sodded lane that leads from the town to that now memorable hill.

The Lutheran Theological Seminary was built on the northwestern edge of Gettysburg in 1826.

Tillie's account of her life in Gettysburg only briefly mentions these peaceful, pleasant times. Her story really begins in June 1863, when war was on its way to her hometown.

CHAPTER 1
The Shrivers and the Pierces

TILLIE PIERCE LIVED ON BALTIMORE STREET ONLY THREE BLOCKS FROM THE DIAMOND. Next door, George and Hettie Shriver and their two little girls made a home. A narrow, open space lay between the Shriver house and the Pierce house. The two buildings were very similar. Both were two-story redbrick townhouses with wood-shingled roofs. On the main floor in each house were two large rooms: a parlor (for guests) and a sitting room, where the family members spent most of their time together. All the bedrooms were on the second floor. Both houses had an attic, or garret. Windows on the ends of each house allowed the residents to peek into each other's garret. Each property had a small backyard that faced the South Mountain to the west. The two families would become dramatically entwined in July 1863.

George Washington Shriver and Henrietta (Hettie) Weikert Shriver were Tillie's next-door neighbors on Baltimore Street in Gettysburg.

George and Hettie had two daughters, Sadie (left) and Mollie (right).

THE SHRIVERS

HENRIETTA (HETTIE) WEIKERT WAS ONE OF JACOB AND SARAH WEIKERT'S THIRTEEN CHILDREN. They lived on a large farm on Taneytown Road, 3 miles (4.8 kilometers) south of Gettysburg. George Washington Shriver also grew up on his family's farm, only 2 miles (3.2 km) from Hettie's farm. On January 23, 1855, when they were both eighteen years old, George and Hettie were married.

The couple moved into the farmhouse south of Gettysburg that George had inherited when he was sixteen. Their daughter Sarah (Sadie) was born in November 1855, and two years later, Mary (Mollie) joined them. George decided that he wanted to move his family off the farm and build a house and a business in Gettysburg, not far from the Diamond. He started construction early in 1860.

Gettysburg was a growing town. It had three newspapers, a telegraph office, a railroad, and many businesses and shops. George's idea was to build a saloon and a bowling alley, just the kind of recreational activities the men of Gettysburg would enjoy. He called it Shriver's Saloon & Ten-Pin Alley. The saloon was built in the basement of his house, its entrance in the back through the backyard. The two-lane bowling alley was built in the backyard too. The main part of the house was reserved for the family.

Way at the back of the yard was the outhouse. (Indoor plumbing was not available in Gettysburg at the time.) It was a long walk to the outhouse in the winter, but during hot summers, the smell of the outhouse seldom reached the house. A chamber pot, one in each bedroom, was used inside the house to avoid the trek to the outhouse at night. It was the job of a younger child to empty the pot into the outhouse each morning.

George and Hettie rented a house across the street while their home was being constructed. Over the months, George kept the workers on track, and Hettie chose wallpaper, furnishings, and kitchen goods for the house. Finally, in late 1860, the Shrivers moved into their beautiful new home.

A Shoe for Good Luck

One of the traditions among the German population of Gettysburg was to place a child's shoe in a wall for luck as a house was being built. The shoe usually belonged to the youngest child in the family. The Shrivers did this. They placed one small shoe, probably Mollie's (below), under the floorboards in the attic. How do we know this? Modern owners of the home found the shoe when they restored the house in 1996.

Tillie Pierce

In March and April 1861, Hettie and the girls got to work on a garden. This should have been a happy, peaceful time for George and his family. But alarming news about growing tension between the Southern and Northern states concerned George and Hettie.

Many people in the South believed that their states should have more power than the federal government to make decisions that affected their way of life. Nothing divided the country more than the issue of slavery. Northern states had outlawed slavery in the late 1700s, but it remained essential to the plantation, or farming, economy of the South. Even before Abraham Lincoln was elected president in November 1860, Southerners feared that he and his political party would force the South to outlaw slavery too. As soon as Lincoln was elected, Southern states began to secede, or separate, from the United States. In February 1861, these states formed a new country—the Confederate States of America—which quickly grew to eleven states.

This photograph of Abraham Lincoln was taken in February 1861. Southern states began to secede from the Union after Lincoln became president.

On April 12, 1861, the Confederate army bombarded a federal (Union) fort, Fort Sumter, in Charleston, South Carolina. The Union troops there surrendered, and the Civil War began. President Abraham Lincoln issued the Declaration of War on April 15, 1861, calling for seventy-five thousand troops and appealing "to all loyal citizens to favor, facilitate, and aid this effort to maintain the honor, the integrity, and the existence of our National Union."

Pennsylvania was a Northern state, and twenty-five-year-old George Shriver at first wanted to enlist in the Union army right away. But he decided to stay home until the saloon

Confederate soldiers bombarded Fort Sumter in Charleston Harbor in April 1861, the first battle of the Civil War. This illustration was created for Harper's Weekly *a week after the battle.*

and ten-pin alley were finished. Most people expected the war to be over quickly. In fact, the original term of military enlistment was only one hundred days. However, the war was still going on when the work at the Shriver business was done in August 1861. George volunteered for military service on August 27, 1861. He was mustered (enlisted) into service with Cole's Cavalry, Company C, out of Frederick, Maryland. Most of the soldiers in this unit were from northern Maryland and southern Pennsylvania.

George and Hettie both believed he would be home by Christmas. Then they would pick up where they had left off and open the new business. George made sure his wife and girls had enough money to get through the next few months. His army pay would be sent to his wife. Hettie knew that if she needed anything, her parents would help out. They were only 3 miles (4.8 km) away.

Hettie could also call upon her next-door neighbors, the Pierces. Thirteen-year-old Tillie would be especially helpful with Sadie and Mollie, who by this time were five and three years old.

THE PIERCES

THE PIERCE HOUSE SAT ON THE CORNER OF BALTIMORE AND BRECK-
ENRIDGE STREETS. This home had been built in 1829, long before George
Shriver started building his house. The Pierce home was given to James and
Margaret Pierce soon after their wedding on August 11, 1835.

Not much is known about James Pierce's life before he married Margaret McCurdy, except that he was born in Maryland around 1806. However, Margaret's family was well known in Adams County. Her parents were
James McCurdy and Martha Moore McCurdy, who were married in 1808
and raised their family on a farm south of Gettysburg, not far from the
Maryland state border.

*This photo of Baltimore Street from 1863 shows
the location of the Shriver and Pierce homes (in
box). Tillie's house is the taller of the two.*

Margaret's Grandfather: Revolutionary War Soldier

The McCurdy family was well known in the area because of Margaret's grandfather, Captain Robert McCurdy. He was captured during the Revolutionary War and held as a prisoner of war. Captain McCurdy was released when he was traded for a British prisoner of war in 1778. Upon his release, he went home to his wife and children.

Margaret's father, James, was born in 1784. Soon thereafter, Robert bought a tract of land in southern Pennsylvania, not far from Gettysburg. He set up a school there and was a schoolmaster for the rest of his life.

This photo of the McCurdy schoolhouse was taken around 1900. This building still stands today.

Tillie Pierce

James and Margaret Pierce had a good life in Gettysburg. James set up a butcher shop at the Baltimore Street house. He was Gettysburg's second-richest butcher and one of the town's wealthiest citizens. For a few years, he also owned the Dobbin House, an inn and tavern in town that is still in operation.

James and Margaret had two sons, James Shaw and William H., and two daughters, Margaret and Matilda (Tillie). When the boys were old enough, they helped their father at the butcher shop, while his wife taught their daughters how to cook, sew, and take care of a home.

This was typical for a family in the 1860s. The young men often worked alongside their fathers and were expected to carry on the family business, whether it was a butcher shop, a mercantile store, or a farm. Some went on to college to study a profession, like the young men who attended the Lutheran Seminary or Pennsylvania College in Gettysburg.

Margaret and Tillie, like most young women, were busy around the house, cleaning and sewing and learning all the skills necessary for running a household. Gettysburg's girls attended a school for young ladies, where they were taught literature, needlecrafts, and proper manners. In 1863 fifteen-year-old Tillie went to the Young Ladies' Seminary at the Gettysburg Female Institute, not far from her house.

Like George Shriver, both of Tillie's brothers decided to join the Union army. Their father was fifty-five years old when the war began, so he stayed home to take care of business and his wife and daughters. No one knew how long the men would be gone. Certainly no one in Gettysburg knew how close the war would come. Until late 1862, most of the battles had been waged in the South. This changed, however, as Confederate leaders planned to take the war into the North. Pennsylvania was first on their list.

CHAPTER 2

Rumors and Restlessness

Months before a single shot was fired at Gettysburg, Tillie and the other residents already feared for their safety. Many of the town's men were serving in the Union army.

Too Close for Comfort

In September 1862, the Confederate army under General Robert E. Lee was only 50 miles (80 km) away, fighting Union troops at Antietam, near Sharpsburg, Maryland. The one-day battle at Antietam cost both sides a combined twenty-six thousand lives. It was the single bloodiest day of battle in U.S. history. In spite of the high cost, neither side could claim clear victory.

General Robert E. Lee commanded the Confederate army at Gettysburg.

Geography of War

To the people of southern Pennsylvania, the geography of the war was cause for deep concern. Pennsylvania was a Union state. Its southern border was the Mason-Dixon Line, which divided the North and the South. During the war, states above that line favored the Union. Most of those below the line were Southern, or Confederate, states. The three border states below the line— Maryland, Kentucky, and Virginia—had a mix of Union and Confederate sympathizers. Delaware, east of the line, mostly favored the Union.

By 1862 the Confederates knew they needed to march into, fight, and win a battle in the North. The war had ravaged Southern farms, towns, and businesses, especially in Virginia. Confederate army supplies were nearly depleted. The North still had plenty of food and military supplies, which Confederate soldiers could take by invading the North. This would also give their cause a much-needed lift in morale.

In addition, General Lee wanted to show he could threaten key cities in the North, including Baltimore; Philadelphia; and Washington, D.C., the U.S. capital. Taking one of these cities would give foreign countries confidence in the Confederate cause. This, in turn, would mean that nations such as France might send supplies and money to aid the South. Lee also felt that a Rebel (Confederate) victory in the North would force the decision makers in Washington to push for peace. The war would end, and the Confederate States of America would stand as its own nation.

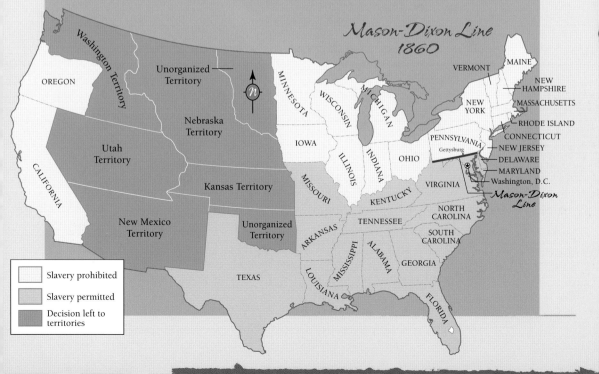

One month later, Confederate soldiers raided Chambersburg, Pennsylvania, only 25 miles (40 km) west of Gettysburg. They had instructions to take whatever supplies they could, especially horses. They also burned warehouses, including one that held ammunition. A resident of Chambersburg, William Heyser, wrote in his diary on October 11, 1862, that "the . . . explosions of shells and powder was tremendous."

In December 1862, Confederate troops won a victory at Fredericksburg, Virginia, south of Gettysburg. Lee's army (the Army of Northern Virginia) was more confident than ever. Southern Pennsylvanians knew it was only a matter of time before the war would return to their towns.

REBEL INVASION

BY THE BEGINNING OF JUNE 1863, LEE AND HIS ARMY WERE HEADED NORTH INTO MARYLAND. News traveled to Gettysburg by way of telegraph and travelers. Gettysburg's residents had been hearing rumors of a threatening invasion for months. Every day, people stood on the sidewalks in town to talk about the latest news. Tillie recalled how the rumors of a Confederate invasion affected the residents of Gettysburg:

President Lincoln (in top hat) *meets with General McClellan and his staff after the Battle of Antietam in September 1862. McClellan was relieved of command of the Army of the Potomac a month later for disobeying orders to advance across the Potomac River.*

Rumors were . . . rife [everywhere] of the coming of the rebel horde into our own fair and prosperous State.

This caused the greatest alarm; and our hearts often throbbed with fear and trembling. To many of us, such a visit meant destruction of home, property and perhaps life. . . .

We had often heard of [the Confederates] taking horses and cattle, carrying off property and destroying buildings. A week had hardly elapsed when another alarm beset us.

"The Rebels are coming! The Rebels are coming!" was passed from lip to lip, and all was again consternation [great alarm].

Gettysburg's citizens asked themselves, Where is our army? A few of Gettysburg's elderly men took up what arms they could and practiced drills. Tillie and the other townsfolk found the old men's efforts a bit silly.

I remember one evening in particular, when quite a number of them had assembled to guard the town that night against an attack from the enemy. They were "armed to the teeth" with old, rusty guns and swords, pitch-forks, shovels and pick-axes. Their falling into line, the maneuvers, the commands given and not heeded, would have done a veteran's heart good.

Besides worrying about their safety, residents feared losing their property. Families hid their valuables in cellars, smokehouses, ovens, and outhouses. Businessmen knew that Rebel soldiers would give them two choices: to sell them whatever they needed in exchange for scrip (worthless Confederate paper money) or to have the items taken without payment. So Gettysburg store owners shipped their goods to Philadelphia or Baltimore. Bankers sent most of the town's money away for safekeeping to other cities. Farmers took their horses and cattle into the nearby mountains or other hidden places where Rebels would be unlikely to spot them.

The Emancipation Proclamation

One of Abraham Lincoln's hallmark decisions, the Emancipation Proclamation (1863), is often misunderstood. For example, it did not free all the slaves in the United States. The Thirteenth Amendment to the U.S. Constitution did that in 1865.

Lincoln did want to end slavery in the United States, in part, for military reasons. He believed that the South would be weakened without slave labor to keep its economy going. Freeing slaves would "strike at the heart of the rebellion." He said, "Without slavery the rebellion could never have existed; without slavery it could not continue."

In the fall of 1862, Lincoln warned the Confederacy that unless it returned to the Union by January 1, 1863, slaves there would "be then, thenceforward, and forever free." When none of those states returned, true to his word, Lincoln issued the Emancipation Proclamation in January 1863.

As commander-in-chief of federal troops, Lincoln had legal authority to make military decisions. In this case, the proclamation stated that federal troops could seize property belonging to the enemy. This included slaves. (The proclamation did not include slaves in border states, such as Kentucky and what soon became West Virginia.) Wherever Union troops moved in the South, slaves rushed to secure their freedom. The army sometimes offered work to the men or allowed them to enlist and fight the Confederates.

Although it did not free all the slaves, the Emancipation Proclamation did ignite hope and celebration. Former slave Frederick Douglass responded, "We shout for joy that we live to record this righteous decree."

This engraving, based on an 1864 painting, shows Lincoln's cabinet advisers reading the Emancipation Proclamation.

BEYOND TERROR

NO ONE IN GETTYSBURG WAS MORE TERRIFIED OF THE SOUTHERN INVADERS THAN FREE BLACK RESIDENTS WERE. Census records and journal accounts from the 1860s estimated that about four hundred free blacks lived there, mostly on the southwestern edge of town and farther out in the countryside.

Gettysburg, like many small cities along the northern border of the Mason-Dixon Line, was an active part of the Underground Railroad. This secret network was made up of people who helped Southern slaves escape into the North to find freedom and a new life. Some of Gettysburg's newspaper editors wrote articles about the ordeal of runaway slaves, describing them as "poor, hungry, starving, . . . wearied and exhausted."

Being so near the line that divided slavery and freedom, Gettysburg's black population kept watch for Southern slave hunters. Since the Fugitive Slave Act of 1850, blacks knew they were in danger of being captured and dragged back into slavery. Even those who were born free or had bought their freedom had much to fear. They could not prove—to any slave hunter's satisfaction—that they were not slaves.

Margaret (Mag) Palm (above) was a free black woman of Gettysburg. Mag Palm was captured by fugitive slave traders but escaped. In this photo, she shows how they bound her hands.

During the first half of 1863, Tillie saw black families on the run whenever they heard rumors of Rebels in the area. They usually fled down Baltimore Street to hide in the woods at Culp's Hill. Some pulled wagons or pushed wheelbarrows filled to overflowing with their possessions. Others carried what they could on their backs. Tillie described what she saw from her window:

[Blacks] regarded the Rebels as having an especial hatred toward them, and believed that if they fell into their hands, annihilation [death] was sure. . . .

I can see them yet; men and women with bundles as large as old-fashioned feather ticks [mattresses] slung across their backs, almost bearing them to the ground. Children also, carrying their bundles, and striving in vain to keep up with their seniors. The greatest consternation [worry] was depicted on all their countenances [faces] as they hurried along; crowding, and running against each other in their confusion; children stumbling, falling and crying. Mothers, anxious for their offspring, would stop for a moment to hurry them up.

Those who couldn't run to the woods called on white citizens for support and protection. Twelve-year-old Mary Fastnacht recalled two black women, a widow and her daughter (wife of the Reverend Abraham Cole, a black soldier in the Union army), seeking refuge. "Mother told them to come to our house, that she would hide them in the loft over the kitchen, take the ladder away and they would be safe." They stayed overnight, fleeing Gettysburg the next day. The Fastnachts never saw or heard from them again.

This photograph from 1862 shows a fugitive slave family on their way north to freedom. Famous Civil War photographer Timothy H. O'Sullivan captured this image.

The Fugitive Slave Act of 1850

In the first half of the 1800s, Northern and Southern states disagreed on many issues, especially slavery. The U.S. Congress tried to lessen these tensions with a set of acts called the Compromise of 1850. The most controversial part of this compromise was the Fugitive Slave Act.

For many years, the Underground Railroad had given slaves a way to travel safely to the North to escape slavery in the South. Slave owners offered big rewards to anyone who brought a runaway slave back to them. To satisfy Southerners angry about losing slaves, the Fugitive Slave Act required all Northerners—including ordinary citizens—to help. It read, "All good citizens are hereby commanded to aid and assist in the prompt and efficient execution of this law, whenever their services may be required."

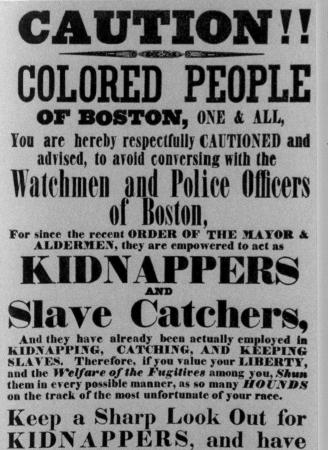

Anyone who refused to help, interfered with a slave's arrest, or tried to free a slave who had been taken into custody could be put in prison, heavily fined, or both.

Free blacks were just as much at risk as former slaves. These men, women, and children often were falsely accused of being runaways, were captured, and were taken to the South. None of those captured had the right to defend themselves at a trial. Northerners were enraged by the law. As a result, the Underground Railroad grew even stronger.

This poster warns blacks to beware of anyone who may try to capture them. Slave owners hung up posters too, offering rewards for helping to recapture runaway slaves.

CHAPTER 3 The Rebels ARE Coming!

ON FRIDAY, JUNE 26, TILLIE WAS AT SCHOOL WHEN SUDDENLY SHE AND HER CLASSMATES HEARD YELLING OUTSIDE.

Rushing to the door, and standing on the front portico [porch] we beheld in the direction of the Theological Seminary, a dark, dense mass, moving toward town. Our teacher, Mrs. Eyster, at once said:

"Children, run home as quickly as you can."

It did not require repeating. I am satisfied some of the girls did not reach their homes before the Rebels were in the streets.

Tillie hurried along the two blocks from High Street to Baltimore Street. As she reached her front door, she saw men on horseback riding into town.

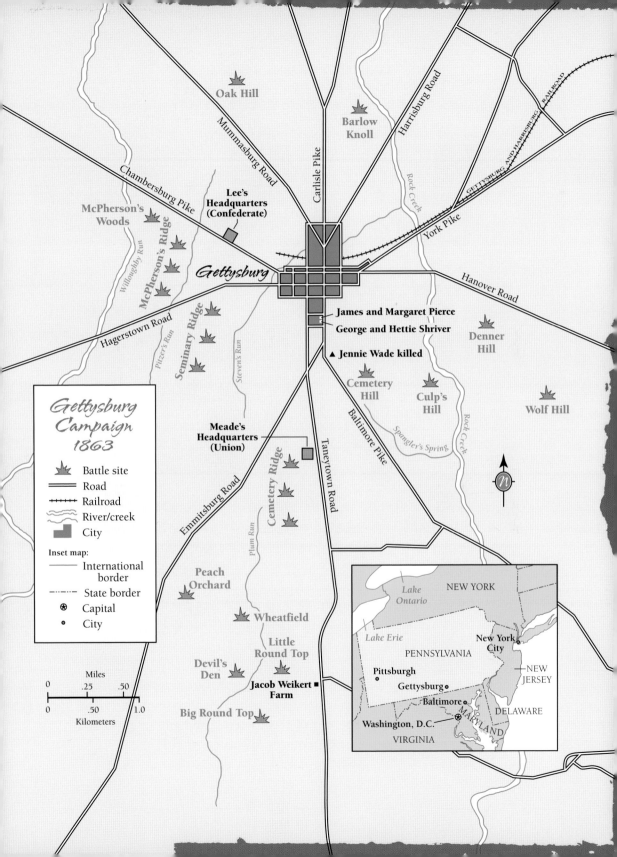

Oak Hill

Barlow Knoll

McPherson's Woods

Lee's Headquarters (Confederate)

Chambersburg Pike

Mummasburg Road

Carlisle Pike

Harrisburg Road

GETTYSBURG AND HARRISBURG RAILROAD

Rock Creek

York Pike

Gettysburg

McPherson's Ridge

Willoughby Run

Hagerstown Road

Pitzer's Run

Seminary Ridge

Steven's Run

Hanover Road

James and Margaret Pierce
George and Hettie Shriver
▲ Jennie Wade killed

Denner Hill

Cemetery Hill

Culp's Hill

Wolf Hill

Rock Creek

Spangler's Spring

Meade's Headquarters (Union)

Emmitsburg Road

Cemetery Ridge

Plum Run

Taneytown Road

Baltimore Pike

Gettysburg Campaign 1863

- ✶ Battle site
- —— Road
- ＋＋＋ Railroad
- 〜〜 River/creek
- ▢ City

Inset map:
- —— International border
- - - State border
- ✪ Capital
- ● City

Miles
0   .25   .50

0   .50   1.0
Kilometers

Peach Orchard

Wheatfield

Little Round Top

Devil's Den

Jacob Weikert Farm

Big Round Top

NEW YORK

Lake Ontario

Lake Erie

PENNSYLVANIA

New York City

Pittsburgh

Gettysburg

NEW JERSEY

Baltimore

DELAWARE

Washington, D.C.

MARYLAND

VIRGINIA

This 1863 photograph shows Baltimore Street in Gettysburg. In late June, Confederate soldiers streamed through town raiding businesses and families for supplies.

Colonel E. V. White's Confederate cavalry (horse-mounted) division came into Gettysburg on the orders of Major General Jubal Early. Tillie slammed the door and ran to look out a front window, hiding behind the shutters.

> What a horrible sight! There they were, human beings! clad almost in rags, covered with dust, riding wildly, pell-mell down the hill toward our home! shouting, yelling most unearthly cursing, brandishing their revolvers, and firing right and left.

> I was fully persuaded that the Rebels had actually come at last. What they would do with us was a fearful question to my young mind.

After the cavalry rode past, Tillie and her family watched as hundreds of infantrymen, led by Major General Early, filled the street. The foot soldiers—desperately in need of food, horses, and clothing—raided businesses, homes, churches, and farms for goods.

Tillie Pierce

The men mostly needed shoes and hats. June had been a cool and rainy month, so the soldiers' shoes were falling apart from long marches through mud. They wanted hats to keep their heads warm and dry and to protect them from the sun on hot days. These men weren't particular about what they took. Tillie noticed that they found and wore an odd variety of hats. She wrote that if they had been in a dress parade, it would have been "a laughable spectacle."

There was nothing funny about how many horses the Rebels took. Some of the town's citizens had sent their horses to farms near

Confederate general Jubal Early

The cavalry stops at a house near Gettysburg in this photo from 1863. Soldiers often took the residents' horses.

Evergreen Cemetery. The owners had planned to get word to the horses' caretakers to drive the animals even farther away when they heard Rebel troops were heading toward Gettysburg. The invasion happened so quickly, though, they had no time. Tillie wrote,

> Father sent our own horse, in charge of the hired boy we then had living with us. I was very much attached to the animal, for she was gentle and very pretty. I had often ridden her.

> The cavalry...came so suddenly that no signal was given. They overtook the boys with the horses, captured, and brought them all back to town.

As the cavalrymen rode past, Tillie pleaded with the men for her horse.

> As I stood there begging and weeping, I was so shocked and insulted, I shall never forget it. One impudent and coarse Confederate said to me:

> "Sissy, what are you crying about? Go in the house and mind your business."

> I felt so indignant at his treatment I only wished I could have had some manner of revenge on the fellow. They left however, without giving us any satisfaction.

Not more than an hour later, some of these same men returned to the Pierce house demanding to be fed. Tillie's mother was outraged. "Yes, you ought to come back and ask for something to eat after taking a person's horse," she scolded them. She fed them despite her anger. Tillie watched from a doorway as the soldiers in her kitchen laughed and made jokes about what they'd done that day. They "threw apple butter in all directions while spreading their bread."

After they had taken everything they could from the town, the

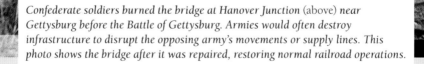

Confederate soldiers burned the bridge at Hanover Junction (above) near Gettysburg before the Battle of Gettysburg. Armies would often destroy infrastructure to disrupt the opposing army's movements or supply lines. This photo shows the bridge after it was repaired, restoring normal railroad operations.

Confederate soldiers left. They moved east to raid more towns. On the way, they burned down Gettysburg's main railroad bridge, tore up the railroad tracks, and destroyed the telegraph lines. Gettysburg was cut off from the outside world.

This well-known photo of Union general John Buford (seated) and his aides was taken by Mathew Brady, a famous Civil War photographer, in August 1863. Buford died of typhoid fever in December 1863.

Boys in Blue

OVER THE NEXT FEW DAYS, THE CITIZENS RECOVERED AS BEST THEY COULD BUT STAYED VIGILANT IN CASE THE INVADERS RETURNED. Every hoof beat, every loud call made Tillie's heart race. On Tuesday, June 30, she heard the sound of approaching cavalry units, many more than before. A little before noon, the soldiers arrived.

Tillie saw they were dressed in Union blue and carried the flag of the Union army. The Union army had come at last! General John Buford led three thousand men up Washington Street, one block behind Tillie's house, to the welcoming throngs of Gettysburg's citizens. Tillie recalled, "It was to me a grand sight. I had never seen so many soldiers at one time. They were Union soldiers and that was enough for me, for I then knew we had protection, and I felt they were our dearest friends."

The soldiers set up camp to the northwest of town near the Lutheran Seminary. Gettysburg citizens were relieved to have Union troops nearby. They realized, however, that it would not take much to ignite a conflict just beyond their doors. Tillie wrote:

> The movements of this day in addition to what we beheld in the few days previous, told plainly that some great military event was coming pretty close to us. The town was all astir and everyone was anxious.

> Thus in the midst of great excitement and solicitude [careful attention] the day passed. As we lay down for the night, little did we think what the morrow would bring forth.

No one would sleep well that night—not the Union soldiers and not the people of Gettysburg.

CHAPTER 4 *Running to Safety*

WEDNESDAY, JULY 1, 1863
RAIN FELL STEADILY BEFORE DAYLIGHT BUT STOPPED BY MID-MORNING.
Tillie and her family had barely finished breakfast when they heard an announcement that more troops were coming. They rushed outside.

> We hastened up what we called the side street (Breckenridge),
> and on reaching Washington Street, again saw some of our army
> passing.
>
> First came a long line of cavalry, then wagon after wagon passed
> by for quite awhile. Again we sang patriotic songs as they
> moved along. Some of these wagons were filled with stretchers
> and other articles; in others we noticed soldiers reclining, who
> were doubtless in some way disabled.

Sometime between nine and ten o'clock, Tillie heard shots for the first time. (The fighting had begun earlier but was too far away for Tillie to have heard.) The sound of faint gunfire came from Seminary Ridge, a few miles outside of town. Before long, the deep booms of cannons resounded, and fat clouds of smoke rose above the ridge. The ground shook, knocking dishes off shelves and pictures to the floor. The constant noise and reverberations of the artillery grew stronger and louder.

The frantic citizens stood along the streets asking one another what to do. Should they leave the area and abandon their homes—or stay to protect what they could? Before long, Union officers galloped into town, warning residents that the town was going to be hit by shells (explosives). They shouted for people to go to their cellars for safety. Tillie recalled, "The sound of shelling became louder and louder, and was now incessant [unending]. The troops passing us moved faster, the men had now become excited and urged on their horses. The battle was waging. This was my first terrible experience."

Tillie watched as tens of thousands of Union troops entered Gettysburg that morning. After the cavalry and the wagons came the infantry, marching in the mud of the morning rain, rushing as fast as they could toward the fight.

At noon, Tillie nibbled at her meal, too frightened to eat very much. Around one o'clock, her next-door neighbor, Hettie Shriver, pounded on the Pierces' door. With her husband George away (he had been in the Union army for nearly two years), she did not feel safe staying in town. She had decided to take her two little girls—seven-year-old Sadie and five-year-old Mollie—to her parents' farm, 3 miles (4.8 km) south of town on Taneytown Road. She asked the Pierces if she could take Tillie along. This would move Tillie out of harm's way and would provide Hettie Shriver some help with the small girls. Tillie's parents agreed to her request.

Before leaving home, Tillie took all her best clothes to the cellar and hid them. No one was going to steal *her* fine things! She came back upstairs and said good-bye to her parents and older sister. She did not pack anything for what she thought would be a short trip. The Pierces promised to watch over the Shriver house.

A Long Walk

WITH CANNONS BOOMING AND GUNFIRE CRACKLING, HETTIE, TILLIE, SADIE, AND MOLLIE SET OFF ON FOOT DOWN BALTIMORE STREET. They took a shortcut through Evergreen Cemetery toward Taneytown Road. The roads were quite muddy from the earlier rainfall, so walking on the grassy slopes was easier.

Union soldiers were setting up cannons throughout the cemetery. They urged Hettie Shriver to find a place to hide before the Rebels began shelling this area. She and the girls moved as fast as they could. Tillie wrote:

> As I looked toward the Seminary Ridge I could see and hear the confusion of the battle. Troops moving hither and thither; the smoke of the conflict arising from the fields; shells bursting in the air, together with the din [noise], rising and falling in mighty undulations [waves]. These things, beheld for the first time, filled my soul with the greatest apprehensions [fears].

When they reached Taneytown Road, the four of them were ankle-deep in mud and muck. The ooze sucked at their shoes and stuck to the hems of their dresses, weighing them down. Suddenly an ambulance wagon passed them, a Union officer's body in the back. "Some of the men told us that it was the body of [popular Pennsylvania general John F.] Reynolds, and that he had been killed during

General John Fulton Reynolds was a popular Pennsylvanian, born in Lancaster, Pennsylvania, in 1820. He was an 1841 graduate of West Point. While directing the Iron Brigade on Seminary Ridge on July 1, 1863, General Reynolds was struck in the back of the head by a minié ball, a cone-shaped bullet like those shown at left. He died instantly.

the forenoon in the battle," Tillie explained.

By this time, the ground was so muddy that Tillie and the Shrivers could not continue on foot. They stopped at a small house beside Taneytown Road.

> While we were standing at the gate, not knowing what to do or where to go, a soldier came out and kindly told us he would try to get some way to help us further on, as it was very dangerous to remain there.
>
> It began to look as though we were getting into new dangers at every step, instead of getting away from them.

The same soldier told them he would try to get the driver of an approaching wagon to take them to their destination. But when the wagon

The little house where Tillie, Hettie, Sadie, and Mollie stopped on Taneytown Road the first day was Lydia Leister's house. The next day, July 2, it became the headquarters for Union general George Meade. Notice the rough condition of Taneytown Road, just as Tillie described.

stopped at the house, it was full. The soldier appealed to the driver, who finally agreed to take the four female passengers to the Weikert farm. The ride wasn't very long, a little over a mile (1.6 km), but it was memorable:

> What a ride! I shall never forget it. The mud was almost up to the hubs of the wheels, and underneath the mud were rocks. The wagon had no springs, as the driver was anxious to put the greatest distance between himself and the battle in the least time possible, the jolting and bumping were brought out to perfection.

Soon the large, gray-stone farmhouse came into view. Surrounded by a white fence, it sat just off the road. A huge white barn stood to the left of the house, and several smaller outbuildings dotted the yard. Behind the property, to the west, was an open field about 100 yards (91 meters) deep.

This photograph of the Weikert farmhouse was taken in the 1880s.

Then up rose two large, boulder-covered hills. These were known as the Round Tops: Little Round Top to the right (north) and Big Round Top to the left (south).

Hettie Shriver, her girls, and Tillie climbed off the wagon, thanked the driver, and rushed up the steps to the front porch. The Weikerts happily ushered them in. Hettie Shriver's mother and father, Sarah and Jacob Weikert, were there, along with Hettie's sixteen-year-old sister, Beckie.

In Harm's Way

ALL WAS NOT QUIET OR SAFE ON TANEYTOWN ROAD, THOUGH. Constant noise from the road kept Tillie at the windows, watching Union soldiers and artillery as they arrived from the south. She saw the horror of battle for the first time:

> It was indeed a thrilling sight. How the men impelled [urged forward] their horses! How the officers urged the men as they all flew past toward the sound of the battle! Now the road is getting all cut up; they take to the fields, and all is an anxious, eager hurry! Shouting, lashing the horses, cheering the men, they all rush madly on.

> Suddenly we behold an explosion; it is that of a caisson [cart of ammunition]. We see a man thrown high in the air and come down in a wheat field close by. He is picked up and carried into the [Weikert] house. As they pass by I see his eyes are blown out and his whole person seems to be one black mess. The first words I hear him say [are these]:

> "Oh, dear! I forgot to read my Bible to-day! What will my poor wife and children say?"

> I saw the soldiers carry him up stairs; they laid him upon a bed and wrapped him in cotton. How I pitied that poor man!

How terribly the scenes of war were being irresistibly portrayed before my vision.

The Weikert household leaped into action to tend to the soldiers. The women headed to the cellar kitchen to make biscuits and beef tea. The Union men would need food and water, so Tillie and Beckie grabbed buckets and a tin cup and raced to the spring on the north side of the house. The girls offered the passing men a cool drink of water. They gulped the water and tossed the cups back to the girls, who refilled them for the next soldiers. When the spring ran dry, the girls moved to the pump on the south side of the house and pumped water into the buckets. For hours, Tillie and Beckie delivered water, bread, and first-aid materials to the hot, tired men and to the attendants who worked as makeshift medics.

By the end of the afternoon, Tillie saw terrible suffering among the soldiers she was serving.

> Now the wounded began to come in greater numbers. Some limping, some with their heads and arms in bandages, some crawling, others carried on stretchers or brought in ambulances [wagons]. Suffering, cast down and dejected, it was a truly pitiable gathering. Before night the barn was filled with the shattered and dying heroes of the battle.

These two boulder-covered hills were known as
Little Round Top (left) and Big Round Top (right).
They lay near the Jacob Weikert farm.

Tillie talked with some of the men, who described the difficult, heavy fighting. They reported that many, many soldiers had been killed or wounded. Some soldiers feared the Union army was near defeat. This was terrible news, especially for a girl whose family was still in Gettysburg.

At dusk the fighting stopped. Soldiers tore down the Weikerts' fences, using the wood to make campfires. As the day drew to a close, more soldiers walked, hobbled, and dragged themselves to the farm. There the injured and mortally wounded were put up in the house, in the yard, and in the large barn—wherever there was room for an additional body. Tillie described the agony she saw in the barn:

> Nothing before in my experience had ever paralleled the sight [Beckie and I] then and there beheld. There were the groaning and crying, the struggling and dying, crowded side by side, while attendants sought to aid and relieve them as best they could.

> We were so overcome by the sad and awful spectacle that we hastened back to the house weeping bitterly.

> . . . The first day had passed, and with the rest of the family, I retired, surrounded with strange and appalling events, and many new visions passing rapidly through my mind.

CHAPTER 5

The Round Tops

Thursday, July 2, 1863

A HOT JULY SUN WARMED THE AIR EARLY THE NEXT MORNING. Tillie and the others at the Weikert house had heard the mournful cries of wounded soldiers throughout the night. Those sounds soon were overcome by the noise of thousands of Union troops filing past the house, heading north toward Gettysburg. Their line seemed to have no end.

At about ten o'clock that morning, artillery units joined the procession. Teams of horses pulled cannons and wagons full of ammunition but did not continue up the road. They stopped across the street from the Weikert farm and set up their artillery in the open field. Sarah Weikert and her daughters kept the stoves burning as they baked loaf after loaf of bread for the soldiers. Like the day before, Tillie gave water to the thirsty men as they passed. But her thoughts were with her family back in town: "[Are] they well? [Are] they alive? [Do] I still have a home? . . . It was impossible in the present state of affairs to expect any tidings from them."

As Tillie continued handing out water, three Union officers on horseback arrived. Tillie apologized for having only one tin cup to offer. The officer in the middle thanked her and drank from the cup. He bowed to her, then turned his horse toward the soldiers in the Weikert yard and saluted them. As he rode off, Tillie asked a nearby soldier who the man was. "General Meade," he answered. The leader of the Union army had spoken to her! She was so excited she ran into the house to tell everyone the news.

Tillie met General George Meade (above), *leader of the Union army, on July 2.*

Soon after, some field officers came to the door. They asked Sarah Weikert if they could go to the top of the house to look at the surrounding fields and hills from there. Tillie was assigned to take the men into the attic. Using field glasses, or binoculars, the officers looked out at the countryside. They asked Tillie if she would like to take a look through the glasses too.

> The country for miles around seemed to be filled with troops; artillery moving here and there as fast as they could go; long lines of infantry forming into position; officers on horseback galloping hither and thither! It was a grand and awful spectacle, and impressed me as being some great review.

What Tillie saw made one thing clear: instead of being safer out in the country, she and the others in the house were in great danger. They were surrounded by troops preparing for another full day of battle.

INTO POSITION

BEHIND THE WEIKERT FARM ROSE LITTLE ROUND TOP AND BIG ROUND
TOP. The Union men who had marched up Taneytown Road that morning passed through the Weikert property and up the eastern side of Little
Round Top to get into position. They pulled and dragged cannons and cais-
sons up the ragged slope. For a while, Confederate sharpshooters, hidden
by the massive boulders and foliage on Big Round Top, fired their rifle shots
down upon the Union soldiers, trying to slow their progress. Tillie saw
the result: "It was shortly before noon that I observed soldiers lying on the
ground just back of the house, dead. They had fallen just where they had
been standing when shot."

The shooting eventually stopped, and around three o'clock, the tremors
of full-out battle began. Everyone in the Weikert house felt the shaking

*A Union artillery unit with horses and cannons poses for a
photograph during the Civil War. Units similar to this one
positioned themselves near the Weikert farm in July 1863.*

This drawing of the Battle of Gettysburg, created afterward, shows the chaos and confusion of battle.

and heard the booms of the cannons. By this time, the Union troops had taken the high ground on Little Round Top. They fired round after round of artillery. With every shot, the windows rattled, dust flew, and the floor trembled. Tillie described it as "so terrible and severe that it was with great difficulty we could ourselves speak. It began very unexpectedly; so much so, that we were all terror-stricken, and hardly knew what to do."

A soldier told them to head east across Taneytown Road to a farmhouse about half a mile (0.8 km) away. As Tillie, the Weikerts, and the Shrivers ran across the field, they saw what looked like an enormous blast of lightning coming from Gettysburg. The light hung in the air before disappearing. "The first thought that flashed upon my mind," wrote Tillie, "was perhaps it is Gettysburg burning." She stopped some passing soldiers to ask them about the light. One of the men answered her, "Yes, that is Gettysburg and all the people in it." Tillie wept. Was her family dead?

Tillie cried all the way to the farmhouse. When she got to the yard, some soldiers saw her distress. She told them about her fears. They explained that Gettysburg was not burning. Soldiers of both sides were under strict orders not to harm any civilians or their property. She was most relieved, however, when they told her that the flash she had seen was a signal, not the burning town.

Even so, they were no safer here than at the Weikert farm. Soldiers told the group that the shells of Rebel artillery units were more likely to hit this area than the Weikert house. With little Sadie and Mollie in tow, they headed back. Shells exploded over their heads as they ran, making them scream and run even faster.

BACK AT THE WEIKERT FARM

THE EXPLOSIONS INTENSIFIED THROUGH THE REST OF THE AFTERNOON AND INTO THE EVENING. Tillie recalled:

> It seemed as though the heavens were sending forth peal upon peal of terrible thunder, directly over our heads; while at the same time, the very earth beneath our feet trembled. The cannonading [continuous firing of cannons] at Gettysburg, has already gone down into history as terrible.

The women baked more bread. Tillie and Beckie tended the incoming wounded, bringing them water and tearing cloth into bandages for the nurses and medics to use.

Through the afternoon, Union troops held the high ground, keeping the Rebels from taking control of Little Round Top. But some Confederate soldiers made it through the Union line and rushed down the other side of the hill, toward the Weikert farm. Tillie and some Union soldiers watched them from a window on the south side of the house. The men explained: "The Rebels are on this side of Round Top, coming across the fields toward the house, and there will be danger if they get on the Taneytown road." If Confederate troops got that far, the Union army could lose the battle.

Yet Union soldiers also had some good news: the Pennsylvania Reserves were on their way. Tillie's brother, James Shaw Pierce, was with Company K of the First Pennsylvania Reserves. Would his unit be part of this battle? Might she see him this very day?

The Other Side of the Round Tops

On the western side of Little Round Top, Confederate and Union forces waged a desperate, bloody fight to control what many considered to be a key position on the battlefield. Exhausted Confederate troops—many had already marched 25 miles (40 km) that day—stumbled and clawed their way toward the rocky top of the granite hill. Desperate Union commanders, including General Stephen Weed, rushed their troops to the top of the hill to take and defend the high ground.

The battle raged for nearly two hours before the exhausted Confederates were forced to call off their assault. The area at the bottom of the hill became known as the Slaughter Pen (*below*) and Valley of Death because so many soldiers fought and lost their lives there that day.

Just then a wonderful sound slipped through the din—fife and drum! The Pennsylvania Reserves appeared, marching around the Weikerts' barn. The fresh troops rushed forward, firing as they ran toward the gray-coated Confederates in the Weikerts' back field. It was a short-lived fight. The Rebels retreated toward Little Round Top, leaving their dead on Weikert ground.

As evening brought an end to another day's fighting, wounded men found their way to the Weikert property. Many lay helpless on the open ground. Tillie described the scene:

> On this evening the number of wounded brought to the place was indeed appalling. They were laid in different parts of the house. The orchard and space around the buildings were covered with the shattered and dying, and the barn became more and more crowded. The scene had become terrible beyond description.

This photo shows a field hospital at Savage's Station, Virginia, in 1862. The grounds around the Weikert farm (a field hospital during the Battle of Gettysburg) looked very much like this.

A Candlelit Promise

In the growing darkness, Tillie carried bread and beef tea to the men, surgeons, and nurses. The number of dead, dying, and wounded was so great that she had to step carefully across the property. As she rounded a corner of the house, a soldier sitting near a doorway into the basement motioned for her to come near. He held a lighted candle, and Tillie could see a wounded soldier lying next to him. The seated man asked if Tillie would bring him some bread. When she returned with it, he asked her to sit with the wounded soldier and keep the candle lit until he returned.

Tillie carefully took the candle and sat beside the injured man, who was still conscious. She spoke softly to him and asked if he were badly wounded. He answered that it was pretty bad, adding, "but I hope in the morning I will be better."

Tillie asked what she could do to help. The soldier had only one request: for her to return the next morning to see him. Tillie agreed. When the other man returned, Tillie handed him the candle. The wounded soldier watched her as she left. "Now don't forget your promise," he said.

CHAPTER 6 Battle's End

FRIDAY, JULY 3, 1863

TILLIE SLEPT LATER THAN SHE HAD MEANT TO THE NEXT MORNING. Her immediate thought was of the wounded soldier, and she rushed down to see him. His lifeless body lay just where he had been the night before. "I kept my promise," she later wrote, "but he was not there to greet me. I hope he greeted nearer and dearer faces than that of the unknown little girl on the battle-field of Gettysburg."

The attendant was still there at his side. "Do you know who this is?" he asked Tillie.

"No, sir," she answered.

"This is the body of General Weed; a New York man," he explained.

For the rest of her life, Tillie remembered his name and told the facts of his death.

Stephen Hinsdale Weed

Stephen Hinsdale Weed (November 17, 1831–July 2, 1863) was a brigadier general who hailed from New York. He led his men on Little Round Top on the second day of the Battle of Gettysburg, valiantly closing a breech, or break, in the line. General Weed (*below*) was struck by a sharpshooter's bullet and fell to the ground. He called for his friend Lieutenant Charles Hazlett, who bent down to listen to what he thought might be Weed's last words. Hazlett was shot in the head and fell unconscious on top of Weed. He died within the hour. Weed, alive but mortally wounded, was carried to the Weikert farm. A monument to both General Weed and Lieutenant Hazlett was erected on Little Round Top in 1883.

ON THE RUN AGAIN

TILLIE HAD SO HURRIED TO FULFILL HER PROMISE TO THE DYING SOLDIER THAT SHE BARELY NOTICED THE MANY CANNONS ARRANGED AROUND THE HOUSE, MANY MORE THAN YESTERDAY. How horribly different the Weikert property looked from the day she first arrived. The grounds were depleted and haggard. Fences were destroyed, and mid-summer crops had practically disappeared overnight. In the house, supplies were running out. Sarah Weikert's stockpile of canned goods and all the flour, meat, and rice were gone. Most of the cloth in the house—from bedding to petticoats—

had been used for bandages and coverings.

The spring on the property had stopped running. Jacob Weikert feared his well would run dry too. The wounded soldiers—both Union and Confederate—were feverish and desperately thirsty. Jacob Weikert could not stand the thought of the enemy Rebels "wasting" his water, so he decided to protect the well, the one asset left at the farm. He hid the hand crank so no one could get any more water from the well. Lieutenant Ziba B. Graham, an officer of the 16th Michigan Infantry, was passing through the yard when the men begged him to retrieve the crank. Graham later described how he had to browbeat Jacob Weikert into giving it up:

> I went into the house, found this man [Jacob Weikert], a mean
> Dutchman buried in the bosom of his family, and his family
> buried in the bowels of the cellar, they having taken safe refuge
> from the hail of iron which was bursting in every direction. I
> ordered him to give up the well crank. He first refused. Just at
> that time a shell struck his chimney, and the noise and rattle
> of the falling brick nearly frightened him to death. I threatened
> to shoot him if he did not give me the crank; this brought it out
> of its hiding place back of the stairway. I went out, watered the
> boys, put two of the least wounded in charge of it and then left,
> receiving the thanks of all.

As before, windows rattled, floors shook, and dust drifted as the explosions pounded the earth nearby. Again advised to flee for their safety, Tillie and the others climbed into carriages and rode to a farmhouse near a town called Two Taverns. The house was crammed with people who had left their homes for the safety of the countryside. Even from this distance, they could hear the same booming, screeching sounds of the battle.

The gunfire and cannon blasts continued for hours but slowed as the afternoon drew to a close. This pattern was different from the previous two days. Before, the bombardment had gone on until dark. On this day, July 3, many hours of daylight still remained. The air grew still, strangely quiet. The people in the farmhouse waited, tense and anxious, listening for the battle to restart. As dusk approached and the quiet continued, everyone began to leave. Perhaps it was finally safe to go home.

The Weary and the Wounded

TILLIE'S GROUP GOT INTO THE CARRIAGES FOR THEIR SHORT JOURNEY BACK. Enough daylight remained that they could see the results of the day's battle as they got closer to the farmhouse. Tillie described it:

> As we drove along in the cool of the evening, we noticed that everywhere confusion prevailed. Fences were thrown down near and far; knapsacks, blankets and many other articles, lay scattered here and there. The whole country seemed filled with desolation.

> Upon reaching the place I fairly shrank back aghast at the awful sight presented. The approaches were crowded with the wounded, dying and dead. The air was filled with moanings, and groanings. As we passed on toward the house, we were compelled to pick our steps in order that we might not tread on the prostrate [collapsed] bodies.

The sight inside the house was no less horrific. Wounded men were everywhere. The able-bodied worked to move the injured to give some room to the family. Tillie and the Weikert women found ways to make themselves useful. They tore any remaining fabric, even some that had been hidden away for safekeeping, into strips for the surgeons to bind wounds.

Tillie was becoming hardened to the sights of wounds and surgery, "else I could hardly have gazed upon the scenes now presented." In several rooms and just outside the house, she saw amputating benches in use. So many were needed that doctors used any kind of flat wooden pieces they could find to devise an operating table. Doors were taken off hinges, planks were laid on barrel tops, and even the Weikerts' kitchen table became a surgical surface.

Battlefield Surgeons

During the Civil War, medical units set up field hospitals (*opposite page*) even before the first man was wounded in a battle. These outdoor hospitals were placed at the rear of a battlefield and were marked with a green flag. The enemy respected the hospital area and did not attack that area.

Surgeons, also called operators, were in such great demand that armies accepted those who had less than two years' medical training. A surgeon's medical kit (*below*) included a tourniquet (to stop bleeding), scalpels (for cutting), needles, sutures (surgical thread), two surgical saws, and bandages. Surgeons removed bullets and stitched wounds. Often they performed amputations and other surgeries, as well as setting or removing broken bones.

Serious wounds to the head, chest, and abdomen usually resulted in death. Surgeons in the field could not perform precise internal surgeries. Men with these injuries were set aside without treatment.

Men with severe injuries to the hands, feet, arms, and legs often received the same treatment: amputation. If available, surgeons used chloroform or ether to put patients to sleep during these painful

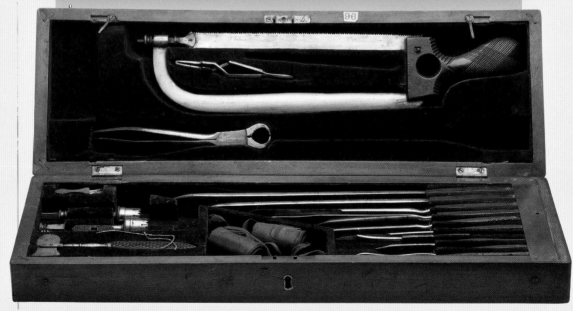

surgeries. Often assistants had to hold down the patient, because he would still thrash about even when he was unconscious. If ether and chloroform weren't available, the amputations were done on a conscious patient, who bit on a strap of leather while he experienced agonizling pain.

Field surgeons became so proficient at amputation that they could do one in less than ten minutes. They had no time to clean up, so they kept working, using the same unwashed instruments from one soldier to the next. As a result, infection was common. Remarkably, only about 30 percent of amputees died. Thousands of men returned home after the war missing one or more limbs.

No one could have been prepared to witness the work of the army's surgeons. Doctors and nurses stood in pools of blood. Their aprons dripped liquid crimson. To Tillie, the amputations looked like "cruel butchery." Her own words make clear the horrors of these procedures.

> Near the basement door, and directly underneath the window I was at, stood one of these benches. I saw them lifting the poor men upon it, then the surgeons sawing and cutting off arms and legs, then again probing and picking bullets from the flesh.

Dead Confederate soldiers are lined up west of Little Round Top for burial following the Battle of Gettysburg. The photo was taken on July 5, 1863.

Some of the soldiers fairly begged to be taken next, so great was their suffering, and so anxious were they to obtain relief.

I saw the surgeons hastily put a cattle horn over the mouths of the wounded ones, after they were placed upon the bench. At first I didn't understand the meaning of this but upon inquiry, soon learned that that was their mode of administering chloroform, in order to produce unconsciousness. But the effect in some instances was not produced; for I saw the wounded throwing themselves wildly about, and shrieking with pain while the operation was going on.

To the south of the house, and just outside of the yard, I noticed a pile of [amputated] limbs higher than the fence. It was a ghastly sight!

One after another, medical staff treated the wounded. Some could be saved. Many could not. Soldiers lined up the dead in rows, covering as many as they could to keep the insects away and out of respect for the fallen men.

Only darkness could give Tillie relief from sights around the Weikert farm. One bright moment came when she heard the men in blue claim that the Rebels had been beaten at last. The battle was over.

CHAPTER 7 *After the Storm*

A GENTLE SHOWER FELL IN THE PREDAWN HOURS OF SATURDAY, JULY 4. By noon, a full-fledged downpour drenched the Gettysburg area, including the Weikert farm. But gray clouds could not darken the mood of the Union men or the civilians who began to understand that the battle was over. This Fourth of July delivered good news: the North had won this battle.

Tillie heard the shouts of victory roll down from the hills. Around her, even the wounded and dying found a reason to cheer. They prayed openly, thanking God for the outcome. She, too, was glad to see an end to the battle. But her heart ached for those who would bear the grief it had caused.

> But oh! The horror and desolation that remained. The general destruction, the suffering, the dead, the homes that nevermore would be cheered, the heart-broken widows, the innocent and helpless orphans! Only those who have seen these things, can ever realize what they mean.

Heavy rain continued over the next few days, keeping Tillie indoors. The roads were muddy and nearly impossible to travel, so she couldn't head home yet. Besides, much still needed to be done. As a field hospital, the Weikert house was busy even after the battle was over. The surgeons kept up their work as wounded men were retrieved from the battlefield. Tillie helped, as she had over the past three days, bringing food and water to patients and medical staff.

Dead soldiers, like these in Virginia in 1864, were wrapped in cloth and placed in rough boxes for burial.

As men died, rough boxes were quickly made into coffins and brought out. Tillie saw the bodies of the dead carried out in the boxes, loaded onto wagons, and driven away.

A Gift for Tillie

After the battle, a soldier greeted Tillie as she worked at the Weikert house. He seemed to know her, but Tillie had seen so many soldiers over these past few days that she couldn't quite recall who he was. He reminded her that he was the soldier who had put her and Hettie Shriver and the little girls on the wagon along Taneytown Road that first day. Tillie was so glad to know that he was well! She thanked him for his help in getting her to safety. Before he left, the young man gave her a gift. It was a button he had cut from a Confederate coat. A piece of gray fabric was still attached. Tillie kept this small battlefield relic, treasuring it the rest of her life.

News from Home

Tillie wondered constantly about her family back on Baltimore Street. Were they safe? What had they witnessed? What would her house look like when she returned?

A kind artillery captain listened as she voiced her worries. He told her if he had an opportunity to get into town, he would visit her family and let them know that she was safe. Tillie gave him a detailed description of her house to help him locate it. (At that time, houses did not have numbers. People knew one another's homes by name.)

The captain went into Gettysburg every day. Each day when he returned to the Weikert house, he told Tillie he had indeed seen her mother and all was well. Suspicious, Tillie quizzed him about her house. For example, she asked him how many trees were in front. He failed her test each time, proving he had not talked with her family. But she knew he meant no harm. It was his way of trying to cheer her up.

On this July 4 evening, as Tillie was eating dinner, the captain came to the basement kitchen looking for her. He rushed in, saying, "Now *this* time I was at your mother's."

Tillie began questioning him as before, but he interrupted her. "I don't care how many trees there are, but to convince you, your mother told me all about your horse being stolen, and that Jennie Wade had been killed while baking bread for her sick sister."

Tillie knew he had found her family this time. He told her he had spoken to both of her parents and her sister, Margaret, and that they were all unharmed. And he had comforted them when he told them Tillie was safe too. The Pierces would all rest a little easier knowing soon they would be together.

July 5: A Walk on Little Round Top

When the rain let up the next day, Tillie, Beckie Weikert, and Lieutenant George Kitzmiller (Beckie's beau and future husband) climbed the eastern slope of Little Round Top. As the three headed up the hill, they met some Pennsylvania Bucktails.

The Death of Jennie Wade

Twenty-year-old Mary Virginia (Ginnie, or Jennie) Wade *(below)* lived in Gettysburg all her life. She and her family resided on Breckenridge Street, around the corner from the Pierces' house. After several run-ins with the law, Jennie's father had been placed in an insane asylum. So Jennie and her mother worked as seamstresses to make ends meet. The Pierces also helped the family by hiring Jennie's brother Sam as a helper.

Jennie's sister, Georgia Wade McClellan, lived nearby on Baltimore Street. She had given birth on June 28 to her first child, a baby boy. She stayed in bed after the birth (as was the custom then), and on July 1, Jennie and their mother came to help out.

On the morning of July 3, 1863, at about eight thirty, Jennie was in the first-floor kitchen of her sister's house. She was kneading

bread dough that had been rising overnight. As she stood in front of the stove, a Confederate sniper's bullet pierced an outer door and then an interior door before hitting Jennie in the back under her left shoulder blade. She fell dead instantly. Hers was the only civilian death in the Battle of Gettysburg.

(Bucktails were sharpshooters in the 13th Pennsylvania reserve regiment, who wore a buck's tail or other piece of deer hide on their hats.) These soldiers pointed out some of the battle's key areas, including places where the bodies of Confederate soldiers still lay. The Union dead and most of the wounded had been carried off the battlefield by this time. Already a foul odor floated in the air and would only get worse over the coming days. The Union army had moved on, leaving a nightmarish mess for the Gettysburg residents to clean up.

From the summit of Little Round Top, Tillie looked out over the boulders and fields below. Some officers shared their field glasses with the visitors so they could take a closer look without venturing into the area.

> As we stood upon those mighty [boulders], and looked down into the chasms between, we beheld the dead lying there just as they had fallen during the struggle. From the summit of Little Round Top, surrounded by the wrecks of battle, we gazed upon the valley of death beneath. The view there spread out before us was terrible to contemplate! It was an awful spectacle! Dead soldiers, bloated horses, shattered cannon and caissons, thousands of small arms [weapons]. In fact everything belonging to army equipments, was there in one confused and indescribable mass.

Tillie
Pierce

Small man-sized mounds covered the fields at Gettysburg. Here and there, a wooden headboard stuck out from the earth. If a burial unit found identification on the dead soldier, they cut the man's name into a plank of wood taken from broken ammunition boxes. It was the best they could do until the families of the fallen could arrive to take their loved ones home.

This photograph of the view from Little Round Top was taken between 1860 and 1880. This is the view Tillie would have seen on her hike up the hill—with the addition of the gruesome remnants of battle.

A Bloody Turning Point

The Battle of Antietam on September 17, 1862, was the bloodiest single day of the Civil War. However, the Battle of Gettysburg cost both armies more casualties than any other battle in the Civil War. Over those three days, about 160,000 men fought. When the battle was over, more than 45,000 were dead, wounded, or missing. Together, these are known as casualties: both the Union and the Confederates suffered about 23,000 casualties each.

General Robert E. Lee and his troops began their retreat in the heavy rain on July 4, 1863. They were headed back to Virginia. The procession of Confederate men and wagons, 14 miles (22.5 km) long, moved slowly through day after day of downpours. So many soldiers, including key officers, had been killed in the Battle of Gettysburg. So many who survived were broken beyond repair. The great invasion of the North was over. It had failed. Because the war's tide had turned in favor of the Union army, the Battle of Gettysburg is considered the turning point of the Civil War.

This painting from the 1860s shows the Union army pursuing the retreating Confederate army in the rainy days after the Battle of Gettysburg.

CASUALTIES AT THE BATTLE OF GETTYSBURG (JULY 1–3, 1863)

UNION ARMY	CONFEDERATE ARMY
93,921 soldiers	71,699 soldiers
3,155 killed	4,708 killed
14,531 wounded	12,693 wounded
5,369 captured/missing	5,830 captured/missing
23,055 TOTAL CASUALTIES	**23,231** TOTAL CASUALTIES

Tillie
Pierce

"A Strange and Blighted Land"

On Tuesday morning, July 7, Hettie, Sadie, Mollie, and Tillie headed back toward Baltimore Street. The previous days' rains had made it impossible to travel by foot, and the roads weren't much better this day. The four of them tramped over the grassy fields instead.

They traveled the same path that had taken them to the Weikert farm only a week before, but how different it looked! Tillie wrote,

> While passing along, the stench arising from the fields of carnage [death] was most sickening. Dead horses, swollen to almost twice their natural size, lay in all directions, stains of blood frequently met our gaze, and all kinds of army accoutrements [equipment] covered the ground. Fences had disappeared, some buildings were gone, others ruined. The whole landscape had been changed, and I felt as though we were in a strange and blighted land. Our killed and wounded had by this time been nearly all carried from the field. With such surroundings I made my journey homeward, after the battle.

The land would be remembered as a death field, where men, mules, and horses took their last breaths.

Tillie and her companions climbed the rise that led to Evergreen Cemetery, where they had taken a shortcut just six days before. It was no longer the well-manicured place of serenity where Gettysburgers had put their loved ones to rest. Grave markers were shattered, some blown apart beyond recognition. A little marble lamb lay atop a shattered gun carriage. Most headstones were blackened by soot from clouds of gunpowder. Human and horse excrement was everywhere. The gatehouse that served as the entrance to the cemetery was practically in ruins. Its windows were broken, and bricks were smashed and fallen. From this vantage point, Tillie saw Baltimore Pike, and beyond it, Culp's Hill. She saw the unmanned barricades that had sealed off the street from incoming wagons during the battle. She was almost home.

Soldiers didn't have the time or energy to bury dead horses. It fell to nearby citizens to remove the bloated, foul-smelling carcasses.

The gatehouse of Evergreen Cemetery was severely damaged in the Battle of Gettysburg.

Home at Last

Tillie hurried up the west side of Baltimore Pike, ran up the stairs to her house, and opened the door. How strange it looked! She saw "large bundles had been prepared, and were lying around in different parts of the room I had entered. They had been expected to be compelled to leave the town suddenly."

When Tillie saw her mother, father, and sister, they didn't recognize her at first. She was still wearing the clothes she had put on six days earlier, now offensive with sweat and mud. Tillie started to say something. "As soon as I spoke, my mother ran to me, and clasping me in her arms, said: 'Why, my dear child, is that you? How glad I am to have you home again without any harm having befallen you!'"

Tillie was safe at last, and she was eager to hear what had happened while she was away.

CHAPTER 8 *On Baltimore Street*

IF TILLIE HAD KNOWN WHAT HER FAMILY SUFFERED DURING THOSE THREE DAYS OF FIGHTING, SHE WOULD HAVE BEEN FRANTIC WITH FEAR. On July 1, after Tillie had left town, Tillie's father walked from house to house asking for supplies and medicinal (painkilling) liquor for wounded Union soldiers. Meanwhile, Union soldiers were racing down Baltimore Street to get into position on Cemetery Hill.

As Tillie's father headed home, he was confronted by a Rebel soldier, who called out to him, "What are you doing with that gun in your hand?" Pierce, who was not holding a weapon, put his hands up and loudly said so. The Rebel took aim anyway, and Pierce "threw himself down, and had no sooner done so, when he heard the 'zip' of the bullet. In the parlance [language] of to-day, that would be styled 'a close call.'" The soldier must have thought Tillie's father was dead, because he moved on.

Pierce was unharmed and continued on his way home. Soon five more Confederate soldiers spied him. They asked why he wasn't in his home, to which he replied that he was getting there as fast as he could. "Fall in!" they ordered, marching him up the street until they reached his house. There, the Rebels demanded to search the place for Union men who might be inside hiding. "Boys, you may take my word for it; there are no Union soldiers in the house," Pierce said. The Rebels believed him and left.

Pierce hadn't even made it into the house when another Rebel group approached him and demanded to search the house. Pierce knew his rights and reminded the men that, according to the rules of war, they could not break into a civilian's house. He proudly told them, "I am an unconditional Union man." They told him he'd better get inside his house. He was in danger of being shot by Union sharpshooters who were at the cemetery taking aim at the Rebels in town. The men went on their way.

Pierce tried the front and side doors of his house. They were all locked. He went to the backyard and got in through the back cellar door. What a surprise awaited him there! Five Union soldiers were in his house, each one sick and wounded. The two most seriously injured were captains in the Union army. Tillie's mother had been treating their wounds and feeding them while her husband was out.

SAFE IN THE CELLAR

OVER THE NEXT TWO DAYS, CONFEDERATE TROOPS OCCUPIED GETTYSBURG. Gunfire sounded constantly. Most civilians, including Tillie's mother and Margaret, huddled in their cellars. Many cellars were damp or even flooded from the recent rain. Snipers' bullets and flying shells could not reach them underground. After dark, when the fighting had stopped, people returned to the upper levels of their homes.

On the first night of the battle, after the shooting had stopped, Tillie's father made several trips up to the garret to look out. The Pierce house stood on one of the highest points on Baltimore Street. From the garret, he could see a good bit of the area south of town, particularly Cemetery Ridge where the daytime fighting had taken place. At night it was too dark to see what was happening there, but he could hear soldiers chopping wood, shoveling dirt, and using picks to break up rocks. From these sounds, he knew they were building breastworks, or low walls behind which soldiers are protected from enemy fire and from which they can fire at enemy positions.

As the battle waged over the next two days, Confederate soldiers climbed up to the Pierces' garret so they, too, could get a good look across the land. Pierce always accompanied them. On July 2, he took a group of Rebel soldiers up there. While they watched the battle, Tillie's father was keeping an eye on the Shrivers' house next door. From his attic, he could see directly into the Shrivers' garret. That day he saw Rebel sharpshooters knocking out bricks on the far wall. They would use their position to shoot, unobserved, at Union men on Cemetery Ridge.

Before Pierce's eyes, a Rebel shooter fired his gun from the Shrivers' garret. Smoke from his gun caught the attention of a Union soldier, who took aim and hit the sniper. The Rebel's arms flew above his head before he hit the floor. His companions frantically hurried to his aid. Later, Pierce saw them carry his lifeless body through the garden in the backyard.

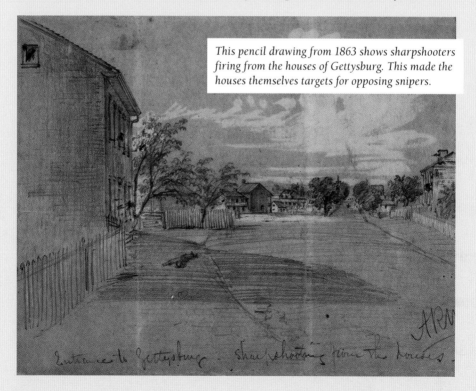

This pencil drawing from 1863 shows sharpshooters firing from the houses of Gettysburg. This made the houses themselves targets for opposing snipers.

Written in Blood

In the 1990s, husband and wife Del and Nancie Gudmestad bought the old Shriver house, intending to restore it as it had been in 1863. (You can read more about the restoration at www.shriverhouse.org.) They had read Tillie Pierce Alleman's book. They knew the story of the sharpshooters in the attic and were eager to see what evidence they could find there to back up the tale.

First, they found the holes (called loopholes) that the Rebels had knocked out in the south wall (*below*). The Gudmestads then pulled up the floorboards under that area and discovered six Civil War cartridges and percussion caps. Three of the bullets were in perfect condition, including the gunpowder! Two of the bullets were Confederate, and one was a Union minié ball. The Gudmestads found other items under the floorboards, including medical supplies. But the most exciting discovery came in 2006.

That year the Gudmestads called in forensic experts from the Niagara Falls (New York) CSI (crime scene investigation) unit. The experts darkened the attic as much as possible. Then they sprayed the floor under and around the loopholes with a substance that detects blood residue. Over an area 6 feet (1.8 m) in diameter, areas glowed a soft, greenish color. Several bright green spots indicated blood splatter. A larger area glowed too, showing what looked like a wiping motion, as if someone had tried to clean the blood from the floor. Here was scientific evidence that the story told by Tillie's father of sniper fire and death in the Shriver home was indeed factual.

An amazing amount of sniper fire hit buildings in Gettysburg. When Tillie returned home after the battle, she saw its effects on her home on Baltimore Street:

> On account of this position occupied by the rebel sharpshooters, a continual firing was drawn toward our house; and to this day no less than seventeen bullet holes can be seen on the upper balcony. One of the bullets cut a perfectly even hole through a pane of glass. The back porch down stairs, the fences and other places, were also riddled; showing how promptly and energetically the Union boys replied, when once they detected the whereabouts of the enemy.
>
> The greatest wonder is, that our men did not send a shell into that house, after they detected the rebel firing.

Left Behind

ON JULY 4, THE PIERCES HEARD THEIR FRONT DOORBELL RING. They had heard no other sound all morning, no gunfire, no cannons firing. Should they answer the door? Was it a Rebel trick? Pierce took a chance and opened the door.

On the doorstep stood the family's Methodist minister. "Do you think the rascals have gone?" he asked. Everyone in town was asking that question.

"The rascals" were indeed gone, but they had left behind many of their wounded and a good number of deserters who would become prisoners of war. More than twenty thousand wounded soldiers were left behind, and many stayed for several months before being well enough to go home or be moved.

The town of Gettysburg became an infirmary for both the gray- and the blue-coated men who had fought here. Many houses, including the Pierce and Shriver homes, were used as hospitals. They were identified as medical stations by a red flag or cloth hanging from a window.

For many months after the battle, disease permeated Gettysburg. The nearly 160,000 soldiers involved in the battle and their seventy thousand horses produced a staggering amount of sewage. Add to that the filth caused by the thousands of dead animals and men whose blood and decay seeped into the earth, mixing with groundwater below. Water from area streams and wells became undrinkable.

Because the Rebels had destroyed the area's railroad line, no one could ship large quantities of supplies to Gettysburg. For this reason, food and other everyday items were scarce. Even so, the federal government's U.S. Sanitary Commission came in quickly, bringing wagonloads of needed materials. On July 7, the commission set up its work in the Fahnestock store

Workers bustle around the offices of the U.S. Sanitary Commission in Gettysburg in July 1863. The offices were in the Fahnestock store (below) on Baltimore Street.

on Baltimore Street. People from all over the North donated supplies to Gettysburg, including water, clothing, medical supplies, ice, meat, vegetables, butter, eggs, coffee, and more.

With supplies at hand, both the Pierces and the Shrivers housed wounded men for several weeks. When the men were well enough to be moved, they were taken about a mile (1.6 km) east of Gettysburg to Camp Letterman, which functioned as a general hospital. For months, Tillie and her mother and sister often visited the hospital to help in any way they could. They brought items they hoped would cheer the men: baskets filled with fruit, jellies, rolls, cakes, and flowers. Some women in town read to the soldiers to take their minds off their pain—both physical and mental. Churches provided services, singing, and prayers.

Through the humid summer and well into the fall, thousands of soldiers found their healing or their deaths in the large, open tents at Camp Letterman. Tillie described the scene:

> This [Camp Letterman] was a large collection of tents, regularly laid out in Camp style.
>
> As we passed along the Camp streets we could look into the open tents, and behold the row of cots on either side. Upon these couches lay the sufferers who, a short while before, had endured the terrors of battle, and were now hovering on the verge of Eternity. . . .
>
> Many sad and touching scenes were here witnessed. Many a kind and affectionate father; many a fond and loving mother; many a devoted wife faithful unto death; many a tender and gentle sister, wiped the moisture of death from the blanched [white] forehead of the dying hero, as they eagerly leaned forward to catch the last message of love, or to hear the announcement of a victory greater than that of death.

Tillie
Pierce

A Town Long Remembered

BEFORE JULY 1, 1863, FEW AMERICANS HAD HEARD OF GETTYSBURG. Before the month was over, however, a nation recognized the place—and its people—as a symbol of sacrifice, duty, and honor. The residents of Gettysburg had gone to battle and had tended to the thousands of soldiers who were wounded and who died in their hometown. Among these citizens was a fifteen-year-old girl named Tillie Pierce.

This photo of Baltimore Street was taken on November 19, 1863, a few minutes before President Lincoln rode down the street on his way to dedicate Gettysburg National Cemetery—and deliver the Gettysburg Address.

Lincoln's Gettysburg Address

The city and battlefields of Gettysburg captured the nation's heart and imagination. Not long after the battle, Americans began making pilgrimages to the site where so many had lost their lives. Tourists of a sort, they wanted to see the massive boulders, the Round Tops, Cemetery Hill, Culp's Hill, and the wheat field. The citizens of Gettysburg recognized a need to honor the men who had fought there. They wanted to find an honorable way to deal with the large number of bodies that had been hastily buried in various fields and woods during the battle. Families wanted their loved ones in marked graves where they could come to mourn.

In response, the Commonwealth of Pennsylvania chose an area and bought land near the town's Evergreen Cemetery. The new national cemetery (*modern photo shown below*) would embrace thirty-five hundred bodies of the Gettysburg dead, mostly Union soldiers. Reinterment, or reburial, from the fields to the new cemetery began in October 1863.

On November 19, 1863, the town hosted a ceremony to dedicate the land and to commemorate the sacrifice of the men who had died at the Battle of Gettysburg. On this day, a large procession started at Gettysburg's Diamond and passed down Baltimore Street, right in front of the Pierce and Shriver houses. From there, the procession continued to the site of the new cemetery.

About twenty thousand people came to hear two revered speakers honor the people and the place. These men were Edward Everett—the nation's best-known orator at the time—and President Abraham Lincoln *(below in circle, prior to his speech at Gettysburg)*. Everett spoke first— and for more than two hours. Then President Lincoln stood, unfolded two sheets of paper, and read his prepared piece. It was 273 words long and lasted three minutes, including the five times he had to stop for applause. Afterward, he thought the speech was a failure. It was, instead, immortal. It is still memorized and recited 150 years later. We know it as the Gettysburg Address.

The Gettysburg Address

Four score and seven years ago our fathers brought forth on this continent a new nation, conceived in liberty, and dedicated to the proposition that all men are created equal.

Now we are engaged in a great civil war, testing whether that nation, or any nation, so conceived and so dedicated, can long endure. We are met on a great battle field of that war. We have come to dedicate a portion of that field, as a final resting place for those who here gave their lives that that nation might live. It is altogether fitting and proper that we should do this.

But, in a larger sense, we can not dedicate, we can not consecrate, we can not hallow this ground. The brave men, living and dead, who struggled here, have consecrated it, far above our poor power to add or detract. The world will little note, nor long remember what we say here, but it can never forget what they did here. It is for us the living, rather, to be dedicated here to the unfinished work which they who fought here have thus far so nobly advanced. It is rather for us to be here dedicated to the great task remaining before us—that from these honored dead we take increased devotion to that cause for which they gave the last full measure of devotion—that we here highly resolve that these dead shall not have died in vain—that this nation, under God, shall have a new birth of freedom—and that government of the people, by the people, for the people, shall not perish from the earth.

—Abraham Lincoln, November 19, 1863

Executive Mansion,

Washington, _____, 186 .

Four score and seven years ago our fathers brought forth, upon this continent, a new nation, conceived in liberty, and dedicated to the proposition that "all men are created equal"

Now we are engaged in a great civil war, testing whether that nation, or any nation so conceived, and so dedicated, can long endure. We are met on a great battle field of that war. We have come to dedicate a portion of it, as a final resting place for those who died here, that the nation might live. This we may, in all propriety do. But, in a larger sense, we can not dedicate— we can not consecrate— we can not hallow, this ground— The brave men, living and dead, who struggled here, have hallowed it, far above our poor power to add or detract. The world will little note, nor long remember what we say here; while it can never forget what they did here.

It is rather for us, the living, ~~we here be your~~ to ~~stand here,~~

A version of the first part of the Gettysburg Address, in Lincoln's handwriting. Only five copies of his handwritten address are known to exist. This is the Nicolay copy.

After the War

THE PIERCE FAMILY

MATILDA (TILLIE) PIERCE married Horace Alleman, a lawyer, on September 28, 1871, and moved to Selinsgrove, Pennsylvania. They had three children. Her family lived in one of the most elegant houses in town, the Governor Simon Snyder Mansion, which still stands.

Tillie was active in her church and was a leader in collecting money to restore Selinsgrove after massive fires destroyed much of the town in 1872 and 1874. After many requests for her to do so, Tillie wrote her account of

Tillie Pierce Alleman as an adult

the Battle of Gettysburg, which was published in 1889. She died March 15, 1914, and is buried with her husband in Trinity Lutheran Cemetery in Selinsgrove.

MARGARET PIERCE, Tillie's mother, died on December 9, 1881, at the age of seventy-two. She is buried in Gettysburg's Evergreen Cemetery.

JAMES PIERCE, Tillie's father, died on February 5, 1896, at the age of eighty-nine. He is buried in Evergreen Cemetery.

WILLIAM H. PIERCE, the elder of Tillie's brothers, survived the Civil War. Afterward, he took over his father's business, married Helen Grace, and raised a family in Gettysburg. He, his wife, and an infant daughter are buried in Evergreen Cemetery.

JAMES SHAW PIERCE, Tillie's other brother, survived the Civil War and was a prisoner of war for a short time. He became a government clerk; moved to Washington, D.C.; married; and raised a family there.

MARGARET PIERCE, Tillie's sister, died of tuberculosis at the age of twenty-one. She is buried in Evergreen Cemetery.

THE SHRIVER FAMILY

GEORGE WASHINGTON SHRIVER, a corporal, came home for a short leave during the Christmas 1863 holiday. A month later, he was captured by the Confederates and eventually put in Andersonville, an infamous prison camp in Georgia. He died there of starvation and scurvy on August 25, 1864. His wife, Hettie, did not find out about his death until December 13, 1864. His grave at Andersonville Cemetery (No. 6,816) bears his name and rank.

HENRIETTA (HETTIE) SHRIVER gave up her house on Baltimore Street after marrying Daniel Pittenturf in July 1866. She had two more daughters,

Lillie Mae and Emma. Emma died when she was one month old. Hettie and her family moved to Annapolis, Maryland, in the early 1870s. Hettie died in 1916.

SARAH (SADIE) SHRIVER died of consumption (tuberculosis) on November 6, 1874. She was eighteen years old. She was buried in Evergreen Cemetery but did not have a headstone until November 20, 2011. On that date—Sadie's birthday—a group of donors from the Shriver House Museum in Gettysburg dedicated a grave marker they had purchased for her.

The Horrors of Andersonville

Union soldiers who were taken prisoner during the Civil War usually ended up in a stockade, or prison. The most infamous was Andersonville in southwestern Georgia. It was hastily built when the prison near Richmond, Virginia, was overwhelmed with expense and security issues.

Andersonville was set up to house about ten thousand men, but by July 1864, more than thirty-two thousand prisoners filled the 26-acre (10.5-hectare) property. A 20-foot (6.1 m) wall enclosed the place. About 15 feet (4.6 m) inside the wall was a kind of fence with a railing that ran around the entire inner area. It was called a deadline because any prisoner who so much as put a hand across the railing was shot by watching guards.

No barracks or other housing structures existed. The only tents on the grounds served as the camp's hospital, but these were near the unsanitary latrines (toilets). One slow-moving stream ran through the area, and soon it was contaminated from the filth of bathing and excrement. Night and day, the prisoners were completely exposed to sun, rain, lightning, and other elements. The South had little in the way of provisions for their own men, so prisoners received even less. Once a day, at three or four o'clock in the afternoon, they received rations, usually corn bread (made from low-quality cornmeal), mealy (insect-laden) beans, rice, and bacon—much of it unfit to eat. The prisoners suffered from dysentery, an intestinal disease, as well as malaria, exposure, and scurvy (a disease due to lack of vitamin C). George Shriver died of scurvy and probably had other ailments too.

MARY (MOLLIE) SHRIVER married William Stallsmith on December 1, 1878. They moved into Mollie's childhood home on Baltimore Street. Like her sister, Mollie also died of consumption. She was only twenty-two years old when she died on July 16, 1880. She and her husband are buried in Evergreen Cemetery.

JACOB AND SARAH WEIKERT, Hettie's parents, are buried in Evergreen Cemetery. Sarah died in 1877 at the age of seventy-two. Jacob died a year later in 1878 at the age of eighty-one.

Andersonville was in operation until the end of the war in April 1865. Of the more than forty-five thousand Union soldiers held at the prison camp, almost 30 percent—thirteen thousand men—died there.

Photographer A. J. Riddle of Macon, Georgia, shot this elevated view of Andersonville during his visit to the camp on August 17, 1864. The photo shows the hospital tents with the open-air latrines in the foreground.

TAKING TILLIE'S PATH AN ACTIVITY USING GOOGLE EARTH

Work with an adult, a friend, or a classmate to download the Google Earth application for a walk through modern Gettysburg—where much of what Tillie saw still exists. Follow the walk below or type any of the sites into the search field to learn more. This is a great way to experience history through technology.

A WALK TO TILLIE'S HOUSE

Type in Gettysburg, PA in the search field. Drag the orange icon to the red dot that is Gettysburg to get to street level on Lincoln Square. You will be facing north as you look up the street. Adjust so that you are facing south.

Click on the yellow street line to move forward (south) along Baltimore Street (PA 116). Read the streets names (superimposed over the image) to see where you are on Baltimore Street. You will also see addresses at the top right corner of the image.

When you get to Breckenridge Street, look for a two-story brick house at 301 Baltimore Street, on the southwest corner. Click forward until you are in front of that house. It has a dark green door and two trees out front. This is Tillie Pierce's house (*right*). Tillie's walk began from this front door on July 1, 1863.

THE SHRIVER HOUSE

Continue south to the house with the blue shutters, just two doors down. This is the Shriver House, where Hettie, Sadie, and Mollie Shriver lived. (The house that currently stands between the two did not exist in 1863. Mr. Pierce really could see from his attic window into the attic at the Shrivers' house.)

THE ROUTE TO THE JACOB WEIKERT FARM

Return to the street, facing south. You are going to take the same path Tillie, Hettie, Sadie, and Mollie took when they fled to the Jacob Weikert farm on Taneytown Road. As you take the path, you can click on any of the icons to look at present-day surroundings. But keep in mind that in 1863 this was a challenging walk over rough roads.

JENNIE WADE'S HOUSE

After passing Steinwehr Avenue, you will see a large hotel on your left. On the right side of the hotel is the Jennie Wade House. Jennie was killed as she was making bread here on July 2, 1863.

Evergreen Cemetery

Continue south on Baltimore Street to Evergreen Cemetery Drive. (You will see many battleground markers along the way.) Turn right (to face west) to see the Evergreen Cemetery Gatehouse. It has not changed much in 150 years. As you scan the cemetery image, remember that many of the Pierces, the Shrivers, and other Gettysburgers are buried here, including Jennie Wade. Tillie and her companions took a shortcut through the cemetery to Taneytown Road. (We can't do that on Google Earth, but we'll take our own shortcut to get to that road.)

Along Taneytown Road

Exit the street view. On the flat maplike image of the area, turn right (west) and move forward until you see Taneytown Road (Route 134) on the other side of Evergreen Cemetery. The semicircle of graves to your right (north) is the Gettysburg National Cemetery, where President Abraham Lincoln delivered the Gettysburg Address on November 19, 1863.

After crossing the cemetery, use the street view icon on Taneytown Road. Turn to the south again. The wall along your left is the boundary of the National Cemetery property. Keep clicking forward (for quite a while). Along the way, you will pass these sites:

- *Cemetery Drive (on the left)*
- *Several battlefield memorials*
- *General Meade's headquarters (Lydia Leister's house)*
- *Wood-and-stone fences similar to those in 1863*
- *Wheatfield Road (on the left)*

Jacob Weikert Farmhouse

To the right of 1050/1054 Taneytown (Pennsylvania 134), you'll see the gray stone Jacob Weikert farmhouse. Click around the house and the barn in front of the house. This place—the house, the barn, and the yard—is where Tillie spent July 1–7, 1863. A cellar door is hidden behind a large bush at the front corner of the house, beneath the bottom left window. According to Tillie's account, that is the door where Stephen Weed died.

To look around more, exit street view. Click on the blue location icons. (Some of these icons give you a photo of the area it names.) See if you can locate the following:

- *Little Round Top*
- *Big Round Top*
- *Devil's Den*
- *The fields across the street (east) from the Weikert farm, where Tillie and the Weikerts fled on the third day of battle*

Write a journal entry about your Google Earth Gettysburg journey. What was your trip like? How might it have been different for Tillie? How long does the trip feel to you? What did you learn about Gettysburg on this trip? Share your experience with your friends and your classmates. Maybe you can create your own Google Earth walk!

SOURCE NOTES

10–11 Tillie (Pierce) Alleman, *At Gettysburg: Or, What a Girl Saw and Heard of the Battle, A True Narrative* (New York: W. Lake Borland, 1889), 10–11.

11 Ibid., 11–12.

15 "By the President of the United States: Proclamation," *Harper's Weekly,* April 27, 1861, n.d., http://www.sonofthesouth.net /leefoundation/civil-war/1861 /april/abraham-lincoln -declaration-war.htm (August 9, 2012).

22 William Heyser, *The Valley of the Shadow: Diary of William Heyser,* n.d., http://valley.lib.virginia.edu /papers/FD1004 (April 2, 2012).

23 Alleman, *At Gettysburg,* 20–21.

23 Ibid., 18.

25 Margaret S. Creighton, *The Colors of Courage: Gettysburg's Forgotten History: Immigrants, Women, and African American's in the Civil War's Defining Battle* (New York: Basic Books, 2005), 55.

24 James M. McPherson, *Crossroads of Freedom: Antietam* (New York: Oxford University Press, 2002), 141.

24 James M. McPherson, *Battle Cry of Freedom: The Civil War Era* (New York: Oxford University Press, 1988), 362.

24 Ibid., 363.

27 "Fugitive Slave Act," National Center for Public Policy Research, n.d., http://www.nationalcenter .org/FugitiveSlaveAct.html (July 5, 2012).

25–26 Alleman, *At Gettysburg,* 19–20.

26 Mary Warren Fastnacht, *Memories of the Battle of Gettysburg, Year 1863* (New York: Princely Press, 1941), 3.

28 Alleman, *At Gettysburg,* 21.

30 Ibid., 22.

31 Ibid., 23.

32 Ibid., 23–24.

32 Ibid., 25.

32 Ibid., 26.

35 Ibid., 28.

35   Ibid., 29–30.
36   Alleman, *At Gettysburg,* 33–34.
37   Ibid., 34.
38   Ibid., 39.
38–39 Ibid.
39   Ibid., 40.
40   Ibid., 40–41.
41–24 Ibid., 41–42.
42   Ibid., 43–44.
43   Ibid., 44–45.
44   Alleman, *At Gettysburg,* 46, 49.
45   Ibid., 51–52.
46   Ibid., 52.
47   Ibid., 53.
47   Ibid.
47   Ibid.
48   Ibid., 56.
48   Ibid., 57.
50   Ibid., 58.
51   Ibid., 62.
51   Ibid.
52   Alleman, *At Gettysburg,* 64.
52   Ibid.
54   Ziba B. Graham, "On to Gettysburg: Ten Days from My Diary of 1863," *War Papers,* vol. 1, n.d., http://www.gdg.org /Research/MOLLUS/mollus15 .html (July 18, 2012).
55   Alleman, *At Gettysburg,* 71–72.
55   Ibid., 72–73.
58   Ibid., 74.
58–59 Ibid., 73–74.
60   Alleman, *At Gettysburg,* 76.
62   Ibid., 79.
64   Ibid., 81.
67   Ibid., 82–83.
69   Ibid., 83.
69   Ibid., 84.
66   John W. Busey and David G. Martin, *Regimental Strengths and Losses at Gettysburg,* 4th ed. (Hightstown, NJ: Longstreet House, 2005), 125, 260.
70   Alleman, *At Gettysburg,* 87.
71   Ibid., 88.
71   Ibid., 89.
74   Ibid., 94–95.
74   Ibid., 98.
76   Ibid., 109–110.

Selected Bibliography

Alleman, Tillie (Pierce). *At Gettysburg: Or, What a Girl Saw and Heard of the Battle, A True Narrative.* New York: W. Lake Borland, 1889.

Bennett, Gerald R. *Days of Uncertainty and Dread: The Ordeal Endured by the Citizens at Gettysburg.* Gettysburg, PA: Gettysburg Foundation, 2008.

Busey, John W., and David G. Martin. *Regimental Strengths and Losses at Gettysburg.* 4th ed. Hightstown, NJ: Longstreet House, 2005.

Celebrate Gettysburg Magazine. "Civil War Journal: The United States Sanitary Commission." N.d. http://www .celebrategettysburg.com/civil-war -journal-12.html (July 19, 2012).

Creighton, Margaret S. *The Colors of Courage: Gettysburg's Forgotten History: Immigrants, Women, and African Americans in the Civil War's Defining Battle.* New York: Basic Books, 2005.

Early, Major General Jubal. *Report of Major General Jubal A. Early, C. S. Army, Commanding Division. June 3–August 1, 1863. The Gettysburg Campaign. O.R. Series I: Volume XXVII/2 (S# 44).* N.d. http://www.civilwarhome.com /earlygettysburg.htm (July 18, 2012).

Fastnacht, Mary Warren. *Memories of the Battle of Gettysburg, Year 1863.* New York: Princely Press, 1941.

"Fugitive Slave Act." National Center for Public Policy Research. N.d. http://www .nationalcenter.org/FugitiveSlaveAct .html (July 5, 2012).

Garrison, Webb, and Cheryl Garrison. *The Encyclopedia of Civil War Usage: An Illustrated Compendium of the Everyday Language of Soldiers and Civilians.* New York: Castle Books, 2009.

Gudmestad, Nancie W. (owner-curator of the Shriver House Museum, Gettysburg, Pennsylvania). Interview with author, March 11, 2012.

———. *The Shrivers' Story: Eyewitnesses to the Battle of Gettysburg.* Gettysburg, PA: Shriver House Museum, 2008.

Harper's Weekly. "The Surgeon at Work in the Field." July 12, 1862, 436, 439.

Heyser, William. *The Valley of the Shadow: Diary of William Heyser.* N.d. http:// valley.lib.virginia.edu/papers/FD1004 (April 2, 2012).

"History of Adams County." *History of Cumberland and Adams Counties, Pennsylvania.* Chicago: Warner, Beers & Co., 1886. 2005. http://files .usgwarchives.net/pa/adams/history /area/chapter-v.txt (July 18, 2012).

"History of Gettysburg." Gettysburg Foundation. N.d. http://www .gettysburgfoundation.org/39/history-of -gettysburg (July 18, 2012).

Hodson, Jane Hunter. *Bios: Robert McCurdy, 1754–1824: Cumberland/Mifflin Counties, Pennsylvania*. USGenWeb. 2005. http://files.usgwarchives.net/pa/mifflin/bios/mccurdy.txt (July 18, 2012).

Hoffman, Gerry (owner of former Jacob Weikert farm property, 1051 Taneytown Road, Gettysburg, Pennyslvania). Interview with the author, March 12, 2012.

Marten, James. *The Children's Civil War*. Chapel Hill: University of North Carolina Press, 2000.

McPherson, James M. *Battle Cry of Freedom: The Civil War Era*. New York: Oxford University Press, 1988.

———. *Crossroads of Freedom: Antietam*. New York: Oxford University Press, 2002.

NMHM. "To Bind Up the Nation's Wounds." National Museum of Health and Medicine. N.d. http://www.medicalmuseum.mil/index.cfm?p=exhibits.nationswounds.page_02 (July 18, 2012).

Reynolds, William C. *Reynolds's Political Map of the United States*. New York: William C. Reynolds, 1856. N.d. http://memory.loc.gov/ammem/aaohtml/exhibit/aopart3b.html (July 18, 2012).

Sheldon, George. *When the Smoke Cleared at Gettysburg: The Tragic Aftermath of the Bloodiest Battle of the Civil War*. Naperville, IL: Cumberland House, 2003.

Slade, Jim, and John Alexander. *Firestorm at Gettysburg: Civilian Voices, June–November 1863*. Atglen, PA: Schiffer Military/Aviation History Publishing, 1998.

Trudeau, Noah Andre. *Gettysburg: A Testing of Courage*. New York: HarperCollins, 2002.

Vermilyea, Peter C. "Effect of Confederate Invasion of Pennsylvania on Gettysburg's African-American Community." *Gettysburg Magazine*. N.d. http://www.gdg.org/Gettysburg%20Magazine/gburgafrican.html (July 18, 2012).

Werner, Emmy E. *Reluctant Witnesses: Children's Voices from the Civil War*. Boulder, CO: Westview Press, 1998.

Wheeler, Richard. *Witness to Gettysburg*. New York: Harper & Row, 1987.

Woodhead, Henry, and Time-Life editors. *Gettysburg: Voices of the Civil War*. New York: Time-Life Books, 1995.

FOR FURTHER INFORMATION

NONFICTION

Arnold, James R. *The Civil War.* Minneapolis: Twenty-First Century Books, 2005.

Arnold, James R., and Roberta Wiener. The Civil War series. Minneapolis: Twenty-First Century Books, 2002.

Gourley, Catherine. *The Horrors of Andersonville: Life and Death Inside a Civil War Prison.* Minneapolis: Twenty-First Century Books, 2010.

Janeczko, Paul. *The Dark Game: True Spy Stories.* Somerville, MA: Candlewick Press, 2010.

Moss, Marissa. *A Soldier's Secret: The Incredible True Story of Sarah Edmonds, a Civil War Hero.* New York: Amulet Books, 2012.

Murphy, Jim. *The Long Road to Gettysburg.* Boston: Houghton Mifflin Harcourt, 2000.

Olson, Steven P. *Lincoln's Gettysburg Address: A Primary Source Investigation.* New York: Rosen Classroom, 2009.

Todras, Ellen H. *The Gettysburg Battlefield.* Symbols of American Freedom series. New York: Chelsea House Publications, 2009.

Walker, Sally M. *Secrets of a Civil War Submarine: Solving the Mysteries of the H. L. Hunley.* Minneapolis: Carolrhoda Books, 2005.

HISTORICAL FICTION

Bruchac, Joseph. *March toward the Thunder.* New York: Speak, 2009.

Calkhoven, Laurie. *Boys of Wartime: Will at the Battle of Gettysburg.* New York: Dutton, 2011.

Klein, Lisa. *Two Girls of Gettysburg.* New York: Bloomsbury USA Children's Books, 2008.

Myers, Walter Dean. *Riot.* New York: Egmont USA, 2009.

Paulsen, Gary. *Soldier's Heart: Being the Story of the Enlistment and Due Service of the Boy Charley Goddard in the First Minnesota Volunteers.* New York: Laurel-Leaf, 2000.

Rinaldi, Ann. *The Last Full Measure.* New York: Harcourt Children's Books, 2010.

WEBSITES

Adams County Historical Society

http://www.achs-pa.org
The website of the Adams County Historical Society helps preserve and tell the stories of the people, organizations, businesses, and events—including the Battle of Gettysburg—that have shaped Adams County, Pennsylvania.

Civil War

http://www.civilwar.com
This website is loaded with all things Civil War. It offers articles, maps, photos, timelines, and more.

The Civil War Home Page

http://www.civil-war.net
A wealth of resources can be found on this website, including original battle maps, photos, primary-source documents (including personal letters and slave narratives), and book reviews.

The Gettysburg Address

http://www.myloc.gov/Exhibitions/gettysburgaddress/Pages/default.aspx
This is the Library of Congress's page about the Gettysburg Adress. It explains its history and ongoing preservation of this critical document.

Gettysburg.com

http://www.gettysburg.com
This website of the Gettysburg community includes resources such as battle information, current events, visitor information, maps, and living history information (for reenactors).

Gettysburg Daily

http://www.gettysburgdaily.com
Started as a daily blog, this site was put together by licensed battlefield guides who now update and add articles as topics and material become available. Entries cover a variety of Gettysburg and Civil War topics. It includes many photographs and videos by experts.

The History Place

http://www.historyplace.com/civilwar
The Civil War section of this website for students is arranged in chronological order from Abraham Lincoln's election in November 1860 through the passage of the Thirteenth Amendment to the U.S. Constitution, which abolished slavery, in December 1865.

Shotgun's Home of the American Civil War

http://www.civilwarhome.com
This is a good online resource for original documents related to the Civil War.

INDEX

Photo Acknowledgments

The images in this book are used with the permission of: © Kean Collection/ Archive Photos/Getty Images, pp. 2–3; Adams County Historical Society, Gettysburg, PA, pp. 7, 9 (inset), 18, 25, 40; Massachusetts Commandery Military Order of the Loyal Legion and the U.S. Army Military History Institute, pp. 9, 30, 53; Library of Congress, pp. 10, 11, 16, 24, 31 (both), 33, 34, 38 (bottom), 38–39, 42–43, 45, 46, 47, 49, 50, 58–59, 61, 65 (both), 66, 68 (both), 72, 75, 78–79, 81; Anne and Dan Nemeth-Barath, p. 13 (all); Del Gudmestad/Shriver House Museum, pp. 14, 73; © Fotosearch/Archive Photos/Getty Images, p. 15; National Archives, pp. 17, 20, 22–23, 57; © Laura Westlund/Independent Picture Service, pp. 21, 29; © MPI/Archive Photos/Getty Images, pp. 26–27; © CORBIS, pp. 27, 63, 84–85; © Chris Pondy/Alamy, p. 38 (top); Museum of the Confederacy, Richmond, Virginia, USA/Photo © Civil War Archive/The Bridgeman Art Library, p. 56; AP Photo, pp. 76–77; © Roger Viollet/Getty Images, p. 78; Special Collections/Musselman Library, Gettysburg College, p. 82; © Eric B. Anderson, p. 86.

Front cover: Adams County Historical Society, Gettysburg, PA.
Back cover: National Archives.

Main body text set in ITC Berkeley Oldstyle Std Medium 11/15.
Typeface provided by International Typeface Corporation.

About the Author

Tanya Anderson is an award-winning editor of books for young readers. Her particular passion is to create engaging nonfiction books for reluctant readers. Anderson discovered this need when she taught high school history and English. She continues in her role as a teacher and guide through the books she edits and writes.

Anderson graduated from Wittenberg University in Springfield, Ohio. After a dozen years in the education field, she followed her dream of joining the children's book publishing world. She has worked for more than twenty years in various editorial functions for Pages Publishing Group/Willowisp Press; *Guideposts for Teens*; SRA/McGraw-Hill; Darby Creek Publishing; and for her own book packaging company, School Street Media. Anderson has also had more than thirty books published in the children's and educational book markets.

Learn more about Tillie Pierce at www.tilliepiercebook.com.